MW00476974

MONSTERS
Live Amongst Us
Jason Edwards
CONTENTS

ACKNOWLEDGMENTS

If you go through the world with your eyes open and your mind clear, then you become aware that every single person you have ever met, both good and bad has taught you something. But you are the one who has the power to decide how you will let those people and their lessons shape you. However there are also those people who show up consistently in your life, who have taught you the most about friendship, love, trust and the reality of the world we all live in.

I am grateful to have had a Mother, who no matter what I have told her has always said "Well if it makes you happy and is what you want, go for it" She also said when I completed my book "You must get your writing talent from me". To my dear Mother thank you, you are without a doubt the person who has taught me so much about the power of stories and how they shape our world.

I have also been blessed with a wonderful son, who has an incredible ability to walk through life, calmly positively and remain totally unflappable and centred. I love you so very much and admire your ability to just keep going and getting on with achieving your goals.

My world has been made up of great mentors as well and I am so very grateful to them. The incredible Joy Gower, the lady who showed me how to help and heal others and understands people's minds and hearts. So much love to you for all your wisdom and long walks on the beach.

Finally to all of my friends who have repeatedly heard me say for the last 12 months "I am writing a book you know" and never once replied "Yes we know!!"

To Gary, my oldest and best friend, thank you for always just listening and being there. No matter what I have to say, you politely listen to my thoughts and nod in that calm sage like manner, I could not ask for a greater, best friend.

I would also like to thank Tina, Tracey and Lee for their great support. There are far too many other people to mention, some who were in my life for a short period and some who I have known for ever, thank you all for everything that you have ever done for me and taught me. You know who you are.

Dedicated to victims of abuse

I would like to dedicate this book to everyone who has suffered and been a victim of Narcissistic abuse. From personal experience I know just how damaging this form of abuse can be. Please keep going and remember you were not born to be abused, you were born to live and enjoy your life.

INTRODUCTION

You have to partake in your own rescue

A Moment of clarity, honesty and reality

What you are about to read is hard, really hard. This is not a book about forgiveness or helping others to see the error of their ways. It is not about rescuing someone, other than you. This book is all about the cold hard facts of being with and having to deal with Narcissistic people. Speaking firstly as someone who has been a victim of narcissistic abuse, both within work and relationships, then secondly as a therapist, Crisis mediator/negotiator and relationship expert; I am as qualified as anyone to teach you how to spot, effectively deal with, heal from and then avoid ever becoming a victim of Narcissistic abuse again. This book will go against many things that modern day society purports to advocate. It may also fly against everything that you have ever been told in life. My words and lessons may appear hard, but remember you are never going to get the best out of a Narcissist, or convince them to change their ways, or save or rescue them. No, your only option is to make sure you are not in a relationship with one. If you have a Narcissist in your family or have no choice but to work with one, then this guide will teach you how to survive and defeat them, heal yourself and move on. Always remember with any narcissist this is as good as it gets. You may not be able to eradicate them from your life, but you can learn how to deal with and defeat one. The purpose of this book is not a scientific study in how to obtain a greater understanding of a Narcissist, although there are clearly strong elements devoted to the identification of one. This is also not a technical book that will attempt to explain their behaviour, but again there are sections that will look at behaviour, cause and effect. No, this is what it says on the cover. This is a survival guide, a self-defence manual for the mind that will teach you how to stop, defeat, break away from, heal and then never get into an abusive relationship ever again. I have also written this book in plain and clear language as I want it to be accessible to everyone, so please do not think you need to hold a psychology degree to understand it.

So how did this book come about? Having also worked as a Clinical Therapist, mediator and crisis negotiator for many years I am aware that I spend most of my time helping those are stuck in poor emotional states and relationships. When I started to work with people in helping them identify the cause of their problems, at the core of a lot of people's issues was abuse that they had suffered either through friends, family or work relationships. As my clients told me more about the abuse and the people who had abused them, it became clear that these people who were the at the very core of their problems and issues were Narcissists. It seemed that no matter what a client problem, there was always some Narcissistic abuse lurking in the corner of someone's story. You see we all walk around not wanting to see, or even unable to see the harm that others are doing to us. We are told and taught to always see the good in others or thinking that we can change them if they are not nice. These naïve thoughts and behaviours just play into the abuser's hands and make it easier for them to manipulate, control and abuse you. To stop Narcissistic abuse, your first step has to be to wake up to the people in your life who are abusing you and be honest with yourself about them. You need to call them out for who they are and you need to wake up and open your eyes now!! If you are in a state of total or even partial denial about the abusive people that live in "your world" then let this book be your wake up call.

But how do we do this and how do we even know if we are the victim of a Narcissist? How can we be sure? Sometimes it is so hard to believe or accept that it is happening. Well, there are several clear signs which you need to check for which will give you a clear indication that someone you know, work with or are living with is a Narcissist and may be abusing you. But before you do that, you need to look towards yourself first, always remember all great change starts from within.

1. Why you have been abused

If you have ever been abused by someone of Narcissistic intent, then it is down to just two things: -

1. A Narcissist spotted that you are ripe for abuse.

They spotted a weakness in you and honed in on it. Understand this right from the beginning, Narcissists are predatory and they are hunters, this is a war and your emotions, mental health, lively hood and your life may well be a casualty of it; unless you learn the rules of engagement. Narcissists will hunt for people who they know they can abuse and get from them whatever they feel they are entitled to have. They will not feel an ounce of sympathy for you and hold the thought that if you are not strong enough to stand up to them, then you deserve this treatment. They will believe that their actions are just and will hold no guilt around them. They may even firmly believe that they are doing this for your own good and will definitely attempt to convince you of this. The type of people who I write about in this book will not for one minute recognise themselves and I guarantee you if they did, see what they have done as vital and necessary to their own existence and survival. They may even hold the thought of how fortunate I am, as I was able to learn from them and write a book about my experiences. This is the mentality that you are dealing with and need to grasp that concept very firmly. I cannot get this point across enough; they are not and never will be your friend. They sit across the battlefield from you and are ready to strike, hurt and take from you whatever they can 24/7. You are about to wake up open your eyes and prepare for war!

2. You allowed it to happen due to your beliefs.

You may have held or still do hold positive thoughts around the person abusing you and believed that at some point it would stop, or you could help them change. Or you may have even believed that this was the way life is and should be for you. One person once told me, "I allow him to abuse me, as its better that I am abused rather than somebody else". Your beliefs and story are powerful drivers in your life and control and justify many of your actions. Whatever positive belief you hold around this person who has, or is still currently abusing you is 70% of the reason as to why it is happening. For example, many people believe that they can help to change their abuser, as it is not their fault they are this way. I do not have any argument for you either way that it is or is not their fault, however from personal experience and over 10 years of clinical work I can tell you, you will not change them! It is not your job to rescue or help your abuser, it is your one and only job to protect yourself, your family and break away from this person. That is it, full stop. Your role in this relationship is really easy you have one mission statement "Stop them abusing you". I recently watched a great documentary about the UK Paratroopers. When the interviewer asked the training officer what new recruits would be learning, he replied. "We will teach them how to close on the enemy and kill them" The reporter then waited for him to give more information and when he did not speak, he asked "Anything else" The officer just smiled and shook his head "No just that, that is what we do, we close on the enemy and kill them".

You need to retrain your mind around these people, you are not here to help them or support them, you are here to "Stop being abused by them" and I have written this book to show you how. As I have said this is a book that will hopefully wake you up, shake up your thinking and get you in touch with the reality of your situation and the reality is, it will only ever change when you change it. One of your first steps has to be to stop blaming yourself. You are not to blame, so don't go beating yourself up. As you will discover from reading this book, most of the beliefs that you carry are not your own and were given to you when you were younger and by other people. So when I say you allowed it to happen, you did. You allowed the abuse to happen both consciously and unconsciously, but you actually believed on some levels you were either doing the right thing or that it just could not be stopped. Well, abuse can be stopped and I will show you how. This may again sound hard, but let me assure you that you have only ever been abused because of the above two reasons. So when you fully accept and then start to change this second reason and your thoughts, you start to take back control of your life again.

3. My Background

So I guess the big question that we ask when we start to read any book that offers us help is, "Why should we read it and what gives the author enough clout within the field they are writing about to establish themselves as an authority?" So let me answer that question for you now.

Over the last ten years, I have worked as a therapist in both 1 to 1 and group settings. I have worked within the mental health field and I also have my own private therapy practise. I have helped countless people to lose weight, stop smoking and overcome all manner of emotional and trauma-related issues. Through my therapeutic work, I became aware of the number of people who were visiting me who had been affected by abuse. But this was not the normal abuse we read about; this was a very specific type of abuse by a very specific type of person "A Narcissist". No matter what the problem someone presented me with; there was always a Narcissist in their somewhere who had done their best to destroy a person's self-esteem. As I worked with people to overcome this abuse, I learnt an incredible amount about Narcissists and the exact methods of abuse they would inflict upon those unknowing or unwilling to see what was happening. Due to this realisation, I started to work more and more on development programs for victims of abuse which enabled them to, move away from and heal from their abusers. As the

Jason Edwards

work I started to conduct in this area became more successful, all my clients started to make great improvements to their
lives and how they felt about themselves. However, I also came
to realise that I needed to do more, as so many people had told
me that they would always return to Narcissistic relationships
time and time again. So I spent more time researching and de-
veloping powerful tactics and strategies which enabled victims
to feel different about themselves and their abusers. These new
tools I have created empowered victims of abuse which really
allowed them to never return to toxic relationships or to go
back to becoming a victim again. It was due to this success that I
was asked by a friend in the clinical health field to write a paper
on abuse. I started the paper and kept adding to it. I did more
research and helped more people. The paper grew and grew and
eventually became the book that you are holding in your hand
today.

As well as the knowledge which I have gained through my work,
there is also a large amount of personal experience which I have
added to this book, as I have also been a victim of Narcissistic
abuse of the very worst kind. The abuse which I suffered could
have destroyed me, but I used the skills which I had learnt over
the years to set me on a pathway of personal development. It
was this pathway which allowed me a unique insight into how
we fully recover from abuse and empower ourselves.

I have also spent time in professional settings working with and
alongside Narcissists. This close contact enabled me to understand the workings of the Narcissistic brain and how to protect
myself from their daily attempted abuse. Within some working
environments, it was very much a case of personal survival and I
realised that we do not have to be a victim of Narcissistic abuse
to need to know how to defend ourselves. Being able to deal
with people of this nature is actually an essential life skill. I spe-
cifically developed the last part of the book for those who want
to be able to deal with manipulative and Narcissistic people,

even if they have never been a victim of abuse themselves.

My work, learnings and the abuse which I suffered has ulti-mately led me to the point where I am today. I do not see myself as a survivor of abuse I see myself as someone who thrives in life and sets out to achieve all of their goals and aspirations. I have even developed my own Narcissist Radar and strong mental de-fence systems these days, which allows me to keep those who would cause me harm at a great distance.

This book is a culmination of all of my work and experiences and the knowledge it contains has enabled me to change my life and never become a victim of any kind of Narcissistic or ma-nipulative abuse again. I set this book out as an emotional self-defence guide to help and prevent anyone and everyone who has been a victim of abuse.

Now it is your turn to obtain the knowledge that no Narcissist would ever want you to have. It is your turn to break away, heal, fight back and reclaim your own mind and learn how never to become a victim of Narcissistic abuse again.

1. SPOTTING NARCISSISTIC ABUSE

It's time to wake up and smell the Narcissist in your life

This can actually be a lot harder than you first realise, as they do not all go around with badges that they "Hi I am a Narcissist, how may I abuse you today" written on them. The problem is as ever, ourselves and our inability to shake off our overarching naivety and niceness and get in touch with the reality of the world that we live in. You will find that I talk about reality a lot within this book and the closer and more in touch with it you become, the easier your life will become. This has to be one of the first steps and you have to look at the people in your lives with a new perspective and fresh eyes, for it is only when you do this that you begin to see people for who they really are. Always remember the camouflage of the Narcissist is your inability to accept reality and let go of your naïve approach to life. We are told and want to believe that everyone is inherently good and has our best intentions at heart, but this is just not true. Acknowledging that bad people live amongst us is a very sad fact to accept, but it is also an empowering thought for you to accept. We want to believe that the world is a good and safe place and our fellow man is a good soul, who means well and when they fall below these high expectations there was a really good reason for this. This way of thinking will only lead you into great harm and you will open your door to all manner of Narcissistic abuse unless you make a change. Remember the movie The Lost Boys, when the bespectacled, smiling and unassuming Max says to David "You're the man of the house and I am not coming in until you invite me" Later on when Max reveals himself as the head vampire he schools David in the art of vampire protection by telling him "Don't invite a vampire into your home, you only render yourself powerless". This must be your new motto, do not invite and readily except Narcissists into your home and your life, for when you do, you render yourself powerless. If your guard is down and you are greeting everyone with positive and naïve intent, this is one of the great cues for the Narcissist to see that you are ripe for the picking and they will hone in on you like a laser guided missile. You need to become aware and sharpen your focus. A great way to start doing this is to stop naively believing everything people tell you and instead judge them on their actions. When you start to look at the difference between what a person actually says and actually does, suddenly that person can change beyond all recognition. Rather than trust people`s words, you become the kind of person who lives in the reality of people`s actions and stops living in a dream world based on others future promises, or being emotionally attached to your own negative memories. Many years ago a manager of mine, took me into their office and promised me a key position within the company I was working for. I eagerly accepted and allowed my mind to run riot with all sort of plans and ideas. I even stopped working on other business ventures with other people I had planned, as I saw a brilliant new career for myself panning out. The same boss a few months later, took me into the same office after an incident arose within the company and told me that I was to be moved out of that position, as I was about to suffer a terrible fate that would damage my career and the company permanently. I blindly and without question allowed this to happen and accepted this terrible fantasy that they painted before me. I became so anxious and fearful of this impending situation to such a degree that it affected my mood and emotional state. Of course, what actually happened was that the situation came and went and I personally dealt with it myself and I was applauded for the manner in which I handled it. However the manipulation had been played out and I had believed their words to such a degree that I was cleverly and easily moved from a position I had desired and valued, as my boss was playing a greater game with me. For my former boss, it was just a game of control and manipulation, which on reflection were the only people and management skills they possessed. Narcissists will love to paint you a picture with the intent on preying on your desires or past hurts in order to manipulate and manoeuvre you. Always be aware of those people who pay to keen interest in your past hurts and tragedies after knowing you for such a short time. For giving up this information is akin to giving up your power and provides them with ammunition to be used at a later date. You have to keep your guard up and always be aware of new people, especially those who display these key traits they are identifying. Always remember that you do not devote much time to thinking in this way, it may just be a day job for you. However, for the Narcissist, it is a way of life and they think like this 24/7. This is a key factor to remember and I will repeat it, as you have to be so careful when dealing with Narcissist people, always remember "They do it for a living".

So who is most likely to be a Narcissist? Basically, anyone can display Narcissist behaviour, it is not hard to do and there may have been times when we have all been a little guilty of this to get what we want. But we are not talking subtle manipulation and distraction in order to achieve a small desire; we are talking walking, thinking, breathing, 100% control and manipulation of another human being here. This is the difference we are looking for as it is very easy to read this and see Narcissists hiding under every bed. We need to be very careful with this label and use it sparingly, but at the same time not let our naïve side colour up someone's ill intent. However writing off Narcissistic behaviour as just roughish, or they did it for the best intent is also the road to ruin. It is so easy to find common excuses for these people and even shrug it off. At one point when I was so concerned about a colleagues Narcissist behaviour and the effect, they were having on me and my team that I went and spoke to their superior. I explained the appalling behaviour and the manipulations that had happened to this persons manager, who after listening to everything I had to say, literally just shrugged their shoulders and said "Oh well, none so strange as folk" and left it at that!!!!

So who are we looking for here? Let us build up a profile so we can start to root out the Narcissists in our lives. Every narcissist that I have every encountered normally has several or all of the following traits.

NARCISSISTIC TRAITS TO LOOK OUT FOR

Clever

Now I am not talking about a degree from Oxford or Harvard when I say clever. I am talking about the kind of person who outwardly may not always appear academic, although many of them can be and will have achieved great qualifications and positions in life. But I am referring to the type of intelligence that is identifiable from the clever long term games that people play, a social intelligence if you like. You are looking for those who have enough of this social intelligence to know how to befriend you and many others, then quickly able to make acquaintances (not friends, I may add) and worm their way into social groups. Once they are there they, will very quickly alter the dynamics of the group and even change the ground rules of the group to suit their own means. A previous manager in a company that I worked for, would often befriend members of their team either through social media, or the offer of helping them work out private and personal issues. Some members of the team were incredibly naïve and were taken in by this behaviour. Very quickly the same manager started to control and manipulate those same people who they had befriended by segregating them from other members of the team. They did this to play the Narcissists favourite game of divide and conquer. This game for them was easy to play and win as once they had won them over, by showing favour and friendship; they would drop subtle hints about other work colleagues. For example, they would make someone believe that other members of the company acted against them and did not value them. They did this to destabilise these friendships in order to create chaos and destroy their self-esteem. For once they have done this it is easy to play the role of friend and become the rescuer in order to control and manipulate other people even more. For more on how to avoid this see the section on (How to beat the Narcissists Drama Triangle). So, always be wary of those seemingly clever people who appear out of nowhere and quickly end up in strong positions in group settings.

A need to establish their achievements and background

As well as appearing outwardly very intelligent, Narcissists may often have an overburdening desire to verbally demonstrate their achievements. This is usually accomplished by brandishing and using their credentials or their qualifications in order to reinforce why others should do what they want. A previous work colleague, who I would describe as the perfect embodiment of a Narcissist, appeared to be able to summon up any relevant qualification to fit any given conversation, meeting or project. They would do this in order for them to be able to establish themselves as the given authority no matter what the situation. This can hide a very damaged or fractured ego and the constant reestablishment of knowledge either through position, experience of qualification can often be accompanied by a forceful character and loud voice. It is not always possible to examine every claim made by someone who you suspect of being a Narcissist; however, you should start to internally question the validity of the claims of those who purport to have experience and knowledge that covers any and every area of life. In my past, I have spent time with a person who in order to take charge of a conversation and exert their will, constantly referenced their former career in the military, or so they would have everyone believe. As they had actually only ever spent time working as a civilian within the forces and not as they would have others believe, on the front line. However, in order to establish dominance and bend others reality, they would talk about their military experience and knowledge and bring most conversations back to this point of reference. They would even use military terminology within their language to reinforce the validity of their background. This is a key narcissistic trait and highly manipulative as it allows someone with narcissistic intent to create a false background. They also know that it has an effect on others beliefs, who are unaware of the truth as they will then assume the knowledge of the Narcissist is of a higher level than it actually is. Once everyone's reality is distorted they can continue to keep up this false level of authority built on nothing more than a lie.

Gregarious and boundaryless personality

One of the main reasons why we are taken in an almost love to be controlled by these people is their personality. They are able to use their personalities and character in such a manner, that we are almost drawn to them like moths to a flame. This is the real appeal of many Narcissists, they can appear as almost superhuman and able to achieve all manner of impossible feats, or so they would have us believe. They are usually the ones who can hold court with great tales of goals and victories that establish themselves as a great seeker and fighter of truth and justice. However, we have to be aware that these self-generated victories are nothing more than proper gander spread by the Narcissist in order to draw us in. Be aware of those who talk endlessly of their own great achievements, academic qualifications and accomplishments. This behaviour actually hides a deeply insecure person who needs to constantly outwardly re-establish themselves. They will also use their personality to cross boundaries and get away with unethical and manipulative behaviour, brushing off their constant boundary crossing with remarks such as "Oh you know what I am like, always causing problems". You have to remember that this level of justification for poor behaviour is not acceptable, but they will convince you that it is. A previous manager of mine the "text-book Narcissist" in every sense of the word, would unfairly and constantly abuse a member of their team by heaping all manner of unrealistic workloads on to them and smile as they did saying, "You hate me don't you, I'm a bastard aren't I" and then leave work early smiling and singing as they did. Always look for the behaviour and not the way that the action is presented. If you are being treated unfairly and abused in this way, an over gregarious personality and the Narcissist favourite excuse of "Oh you know me that is just what I am like", is no excuse.

They are the scriptwriter and you are just part of the cast

If all the world is a stage, then the Narcissist sees themselves not only in the starring role, but they also see themselves as the director, screenwriter and set designer as well. This is one of the most obvious traits that you need to look out for within a person who you suspect as being a Narcissist and it goes way beyond being a control freak, this is near god complex. You have to remember that you are dealing with a person who can cross boundaries, is void of emotion when it comes to your feelings and will use any tactic at hand to get what they want. They will do this as they only have one priority, their own self-gratification. Now there is no finer way for a Narcissist to achieve self-gratification than by taking centre stage in a play they direct and write as they go along. They will of course constantly change the script (by lying) to suit their needs whenever it pleases them. You must remember that you will only ever have a supporting role and as soon as you think you know your part in their dark play that will change as well. They will look at obtaining such a high degree of control that as soon as you think you have learnt the script and how to interact they will rewrite it on the spot. Why? Rewriting the script is how they keep control of you and everything around them, by keeping you off balance. They will never want you to obtain a true sense of your self-worth for the minute you do, you may attempt to break away from them. Imagine for a minute the actor or actress who becomes aware of their own popularity or talent, what would this mean for them? They may demand a higher fee or even worse sack their agent and work with new people who encourage their talent. This is the last thing the Narcissist wants is for you to become self-assured and confident, so they will redirect, rewrite and create drama, to ensure that you never achieve or feel your sense of self-value. Many years ago I used to see a lot of one person who at the time always displayed odd behaviour. I was less aware of control and manipulation then but knew that I always felt that whatever I said was the wrong thing and their response always seemed to make me feel worthless, without them directly attacking me. As I learnt more and became aware of personality disorders and abuse I started to monitor them. One day they came to visit me and Robbie Williams was playing on the radio. They commented on how much they liked him and his music and their words were "He is a class act, that boy" I remember agreeing as at the time I thought he was a great artist. Several weeks later when some friends were visiting, I invited this person to join us. By chance there was a Robbie Williams concert was on TV that night. I stated to everyone that it was on and who fancied watching it, I added I was a fan and thought he was a great entertainer. The same person who had stated privately how much he liked Robbie Williams put me down in front of the group and laughed at me for wanting to watch it. In front of everyone, he stated they "That is just immature rubbish for children, not grown-ups". I was suddenly aware of what he had done. He had completely rewritten the script to establish himself as the mature leader of the group, while at the same time categorised me as a child. I knew that to strike back and accuse them of also liking them, would actually make me look weaker as they would only deny it. It was at this point that I started to realise the extent that rewriting the script can have. In a later chapter, I will give you the ultimate tool for countering this tactic that will allow you to re-establish yourself after an attack of this kind. Always be aware of what you give out to those people who are not as associated with the truth and reality. The lesson here for me was to keep this person at a distance in the future and not make myself vulnerable again. After this point I noticed just how this person probed others for information, never revealing anything in a group setting. For if they reveal a desire or piece of information it would be so much harder, near impossible for them to rewrite it again with more than one witness to hand.

Life is always a drama

If there is one Narcissistic trait which stands out it is their ability to self-generate drama and drag you and others into it. As humans we are quite addicted to drama, it is the reason why film and television are so popular, they heighten our emotions and let's be honest we love it. We pay good money for it and it's the reason why every episode of EastEnders ends on a cliffhanger? Drama, when played out on the screen, allows us to enjoy it, have that heightened sense of excitement safely and then let it go. It only becomes damaging when it becomes part of our daily life and we can never escape it. Unfortunately, there are those people who are addicted to drama and that addiction can make you a target for Narcissistic abuse. As we will look at further sections you need to be aware if you are someone who becomes hooked on the drama of relationships? If you are then a Narcissist will happily keep you fed with high emotional rollercoaster treats, but there will be a price to pay for this. You will also have to suffer the lows and comedowns and lack of control that you will suffer from the constant manipulation of never knowing where you are with them.

They can hurt you and cry out in pain

Many years ago when I was young, I watched a young girl strike her younger brother in a fit of rage after they had got into an argument. The girl had struck him in an unproved attack as although he was younger, he was smarter and making more sense. The girl who now realised she was unable to win lashed out with any warning. On hearing the commotion their mother came to intervene. Immediately and to my surprise, the young girl cried out in pain herself. Her performance was so dramatic and she was so convincing in her approach as to what had happened, that she seemed to just suck up all of the attention and need for help. She claimed that her hand was in such agony after striking her younger and smaller Brother that she was the one in need of medical attention. She cradled her hand, red faced, tears streaming down her cheeks as she let out the loudest and most painful of cries. Her helpless Mothers emotional buttons now fully pressed in the right order could not help but go to the older of her siblings to offer comfort. She reassured her that she was ok and that she would take care of her and everything would be ok. I remember even in my younger years looking at her Brother who was now carrying a large red mark on his arm and in some pain; thinking to myself, "There is something not right with that girl!" The boy's Mother now drained of emotion and left with only exhaustion turned to him and not showing any sympathy said "Oh you'll be all right, look at your "little" sister and the state she is in" The young girl in a display of early Narcissism, had just unexpectedly exploded and attacked her Brother; as she had not been able to intellectually keep up with him. On hurting him and realising how this could damage her reputation, without a thought she had been able to claim victory. She even reframed the situation by having her Mother see her as the "Little" sister, who was older and taller than her Brother. I often wonder how these siblings faired later on in life. This is actually a classic Narcissist trait of being able to explode at a moment's notice, cause all manner of physical and emotional pain and then cry out as the wounded party. I used to work with someone who for many years was a victim of all manner verbal and emotional abuse by their partner. But on meeting this person`s partner they could present as incredibly helpless and unwell and even claim they were the victim and not the abuser. They were so accomplished at this tactic that they were able to repeatedly hurt their partner in numerous ways and then present as injured to such a degree that a senior colleague of mine described them as "A lovely young person". Be aware of the person who is capable of hurting you and not only saying look what you made me do but is also capable of crying to others of how much pain you caused them because of attack they made on you.

They distort reality through conversation and manipulation I am about to reveal one of the narcissists greatest weapons and traits, reality distortion!! Have you ever spent time with some-one who always attempts to control the conversation and take it in a certain direction? If they make comments about other people are they usually negative and cause you to doubt that person's ability or character? Yet when they steer the conversa-tion towards themselves as they always will, it is always in a positive light. To control the conversation this way serves the purpose of the Narcissist as it allows them to do that one thing they desire more than any other, taking control of the game by reality distortion by nothing more than conversation. Most narcissists can be very gregarious by nature and always at the centre of most conversations. After all, if a group are talking they need to be there to make sure it's not about them, as well as it being an opportunity to distort a whole group of people`s opinions. It is always worth noting at this point that their con-versation will always lack depth and stay on a superficial level. This is because their reality distorting narrative has no real sub-stance or basis in the real world. Also be aware of those people who if challenged on any of their words or comments, fall back on "I was just trying to help" or become defensive or attempt to garner sympathy by pointing out how bad their own life is. They may even go for the classic "I was just being funny and hav-ing a laugh" and turning it back onto you, for example, "What is wrong with you, can't you take a joke" the classic narcissistic strategy for destabilising you. First, they put you down then ac-cuse you of not being a complete person for not being able to withstand "a bit of a ribbing". Now good natured humour is fine and some people enjoy the banter. But remember with the Narcissist they are using a technique that others use to build bridges with as a psychological stick to beat you with, put you down and ultimately change yours and others reality. A former colleague of mine who often displayed high narcissistic traits was only ever capable of talking in this manner and no matter what the subject matter was, would have to gain control of it. They always did this in order to put others down and bolster themselves within the group and distort everyone's reality. I remember on several occasions being at work and the group I was sitting with were discussing international relations and politics. My former colleague who was more than capable of joining in on this, honed in on a person who was talking within the group and for no reason make a very negative comment about them. The comments they made were so wide of the conversation that was in flow that it brought others out of the depth of conversation and stop everyone dead in their tracks. This was a classic breaking everyone's state and reality distorting and allowed the narcissist to take a grownup mature conversation about something the group were interested in something completely different. It also allowed them to succeed in putting someone down and making themselves appear heroic, essential to others existence and in control.

To demonstrate how they did this I will recount their actions and break it down and you can see how the Narcissists greatest weapon looks from the inside.

It was during one lunchtime when a conversation regarding having more open borders in Europe was in full flow, everyone was joining in by adding their points of view, listening to and respecting others opinions and thoughts and bringing relevant experience and knowledge to the conversation. It was interesting as there were so many diverse points of view. No one was making the conversation personal, so everyone was able to defend their position intellectually and explain their interests. Then suddenly without any prompting and while another person was still speaking our resident Narcissist who had remained silent up until now decided to just speak up really loudly and focus in on a member of the groups necktie. Now the necktie in question just happened to have a picture of a well-known animated character on it. They loudly and mockingly proclaimed for everyone to hear "Oh my gosh I've just noticed your tie, are you really wearing a tie with that on it!!!" Everyone stopped and looked at the person who was wearing the tie, the stunned group fell silent. Now realising they had everyone's attention the narcissist started on them. "You are not going to wear that on your date tonight are you?" The person under attack stopped and with a quizzical look replied "No". But by now it was too late our Narcissist was on a roll would not be stopped. "Well I was going to say what would a girl, think if you turned up wearing that. If I was going on a date and a man turned up with that on his tie I would not be impressed. There is no way I would go on a second date with a man wearing that". They continued their monologue loudly and attempted to garner agreement from the others in the group. "What do you think?" they said turning to another member of the group and before they even answered just carried on "It doesn't show you made much of an effort just wearing your work clothes to a date". The person again stated they were not going to wear it, but the Narcissist gave this comment no acknowledgement and just kept going. The first and second part of their strategy complete they now launched into the third part. As they now unbelievably took credit for giving the focus of their attention fashion advice and added. "Now when you go on your date tonight, you can thank me for reminding you for not wearing that and giving you fashion advice. I know a lot about fashion I do. You are so lucky to have me here looking out for you. Just think if you marry them it will be because of what I said and all of these people witnessed it".

Did you see what they did? It was the most incredible piece of

Narcissistic reality distortion and all done under the guise of help and humour. They started off by totally redirecting the conversation away from the subject matter and onto a member of the group. They then belittled this person in a mocking and humorous manner and at the same time put themselves into a position of power, responsibility and in an advisory role. Even though the advice given had never been asked for, was not needed and again distorted reality. They picked up on a person`s item of clothing, distorted it from something normal into something bad and then further distorted it by painting a picture of that person wearing on a date. This action never was intended by the person wearing it (This reality was to be avoided by the narcissist at all costs). They then took the conversation so far out of reality (from a first date to getting married) and through that distortion laid down the foundations that a work colleague would owe them for their future happiness. They even brought the group into it with a further false distortion that it was all of them in agreement. I watched this person do this time after time after time to so many different people. They would claim ownership for so many things that were not going to happen but paint a picture that these things were going to happen if they were not there to stop them and the put themselves in the centre of the picture as the hero. I remember them once pointing out a large and very obviously puddle of water to someone who had clearly seen it and was actually in the process of walking around it. There was even a large yellow safety sign by it. "Watch out for that water" they shouted getting everyone's attention. They then stated "Just as well I was here, your shoes would have been ruined, then what would your wife had said. I'll have to let her know that I'm here looking after you when I see her". The person who they directed it at just looked at them in utter disbelief as so many people did, not that they ever gave anyone's thoughts any credit. I later heard the same person stating to another colleague "If it wasn't for me, he would have ruined his shoes, there was a huge yellow sign he was going to walk right through the water. You know it's just as well I have had safety training in these areas if he slipped up he could have been off work for weeks and the company might not have paid his wages" The story just continued and become more distorted each time they told it.

Just beware of the reality distortion field; it can be one of the Narcissists most frequently used weapons, I will talk about reality distortion more in more depth later on and how we can counter this tactic.

Everything is taken personally and they will take you down rather than lose

It is a real skill to be able to detach from a debate and look at what the other person is doing. As a professional mediator and high-end business negotiator, I spent many years doing just this. You have to remain very centred, have a lot of self-confidence, good self-esteem and want to create a positive win-win for everyone at the table.

The above paragraph does not describe a Narcissist or their intent. Most Narcissists will have an agenda and as you will see they actually have very few tools and skills to achieve this agenda, however the ones they have they are very skilful in applying. One of the tools they will apply when challenged or disagreed with is to take everything that is said to them as a personal attack. This will usually be with the aim to deflect you away for what they are attempting to achieve, by making you feel bad for disagreeing with them. I used to be in a relationship with someone who would always attempt to reframe my words and take things on a personal level, whenever I attempted to bring my own thoughts to a discussion. If I then stuck to my guns, they would act hurt to the point where they would storm out of the room. This made talking and negotiating with them impossible whenever things needed resolving, but only when they felt that things were not going their way. When the relationship ran into difficulties whenever I asked them to reflect upon when they had just said to me, or the actions they had taken; rather than be capable of doing this they would scream "You are just beating me up now" and storm out of the room. If I attempted to follow this up, they would say that they felt trapped and cornered and I was now bullying them. So I would back off and nothing would move forward. This was a repeated pattern they displayed to any conversation we had that may have involved them sharing responsibility for any problems. They took this to such a degree that even when they committed an act of total betrayal towards myself and their closest friends, their response was to blame anyone and everyone other than themselves. When I challenged the fact that they quite rightly carried equal responsibility for this act, once again they stormed out of the room screaming and crying and blaming me. It was inconceivable to their Narcissistic brain that they could ever take responsibility for their actions and instead took every opportunity to align me with any of my weaknesses and insecurities rather than admit to any wrongdoing. In negotiation and mediation, you learn that to be successful it is not a win-lose or a zero-sum game, it is about attempting to move forward together to improve relationships and not blame or destroy the other side. For those with Narcissistic intent, this level of reasoning will be beyond them. Always be aware of those who just want to see any confrontation as a zero-sum game of either win or lose and they will always want to be the one that wins and never negotiates.

They become attached to quickly to every area of our lives
Be aware of those bosses and work colleagues who act over friendly and attempt to draw us into their world and confidence way too quickly. Or that new person who immediately shows up in every area of our life, our social media feeds liking everything we like, casually inviting themselves around for coffee without being asked. Very soon they start to make themselves relevant to our world by helping us out time and time again and

coming to our rescue, as we fail to realise that this help will come at a very high price. It is not long before they are part of our world in and know all our family and friends by first name, learning all about them. Always be aware of this behaviour as it will not be long before this person is attempting to separate you from long trusted family and friends.

By now you should be starting to build up an idea of the type of person that you need to be aware of. However sharp and switched on we are though, there will always be those people who still manage to get in under our radar. This is probably because we don't wish to think negatively of people and always want to think well of our others, as we are taught and told we should do. There is nothing wrong with this, except for when it comes at a price. So now let us take our first look at why relationships are fertile ground for a Narcissist. Relationships can often be the easiest area for the Narcissist to infiltrate because at heart we all want to connect with other people and humans are not by their very nature solitary creatures. For many people, this desire to share is actually a huge weakness and we can even build up a total fear of being alone. This fear, in turn, can then cause us to crave and desire having that special someone in our lives and that can be so potentially harmful and dangerous as we will put up with all manner of unacceptable behaviour, rather than just being comfortable with being on our own. The Famous French Philosopher Blasé Pascal said "All of humanity's problems stem from man's inability to sit quietly in a room" There is such great wisdom in those words when applied to our desire to be in a relationship. After all, if you are comfortable with who you are if you are centred, secure, self-assured and happy to just be in your own company, then why would you seek out another who will harm you to share your life with? Always be so mindful when letting others into your world. Ask yourself are you doing this for the right reason, or is it an act of desperation and loneliness?

You are nothing more than a means to an ends, a piece on the board to them

There are two games that I always believe exemplify life and interactions. One is Poker and the other is Chess. In Chess the smallest and weakest piece on the board is the Pawn, it is sacrificed in order that the real objective of winning the game can be obtained. To the Narcissist, you are nothing more than a Pawn in their game. They will not only let you take a hit for them if it meant them getting what they want, but they will purposely put you in harm's way to achieve even a minor goal. In a former relationship of mine when I was at a very low point, I actually allowed myself to be repeatedly moved and manoeuvred around the board like I was nothing more than a pawn. On reflection, to this person that was all that I was, a game piece, a stepping stone to a larger more lucrative pond. They had so skilfully broke me down over a long period that I could not even see the emotional and psychological damage which was being inflicted upon me. They had an objective, which was to psychologically break me and it nearly worked. If it had of broken me, I would have allowed them to achieve their goals with no care or concern to any damage caused. At the time I was becoming emotionally unwell due to their constant repeated and daily emotional abuse of me. It got to such a point that for me it was getting harder and harder to go on. They were so relentless in their cruelty, manipulation and reframing and redefining of who I was and what I was capable of, that I was ready to break and give them whatever they wanted. Every area of my character and personality and ability they almost systematically destroyed, just so they could get their way. Their abuse of me was one which created an artificial construction of who I was. It got to such a point that I did not even recognise myself anymore as they battered me daily telling me how utterly useless I was. They were so perfect in their Narcissistic abuse that even I started to believe it and totally broken I would apologise daily just for being me. It got to such a point that I would have done anything they asked to bring an end to my situation of total misery and utter despair. Totally broken I was now so close to complying with their final demands and manipulations. If I had have gone along with these manipulations it would have totally destroyed me, both mentally and financially and completely removed me from the table. However, I was lucky, really lucky and at the very last minute, something changed in me after talking with a friend I went to visit one evening. I came to my senses and challenged my resident Narcissist on everything they had been doing to me and from this point, I started to bring everything back under my control again. If I had not done this then my fate at their hands would have been very different and I may not even be here to write this book today. They showed no compassion or empathy, pushed me to total emotional despair and extremes, constantly abused me whilst crying out to everyone else of the hurt they were in. Their Narcissism showed no limits and they knew no depths or boundaries.

That last paragraph you have read served a purpose, I wrote it to give you an example of just how easy even a really strong and capable person is of being manipulated emotionally so they can then just be pushed into any situation the Narcissist wishes.

To this particular Narcissist, everyone was a piece on the board to be moved around as long as they achieved their goal. They showed no concern for others' lives whether they were close friends or family or for the pain they caused in relationships, as they manipulatively wrote, directed and acted out this self-achieving drama. Yet on the surface, they presented to all as the victim to be held close, sympathised, supported, rallied around and helped and those incapable of seeing through their Narcissistic games did just that. Everyone was there to be used and controlled, friends, work colleagues even family. They all fell for the act and like a Grandmaster at their game, the Narcissist just kept on playing.

You need to remember that you are not a playing piece in someone else game, you are a person with emotions, goals, desires and dreams and you have as much right to these as other people. Beware of those who trample on your dreams and goals, redefine you and tell you who and what you are. This manipulation is game playing at the highest level and the ultimate trait of the true Narcissist. It encompasses all of the other plays in their playbook and they play it well, it is time for you to stop being a pawn or a knight or even a king or queen. It is time for you to learn the rules of the game and become a Grandmaster yourself, so step off of the board and learn how to start making positive moves for yourself and your goals and dreams.

How to spot if you are in a Narcissistic relationship

So having looked at some of the main traits and behaviours of a Narcissist, let us take a look at some of the major red flags that you should be aware of if you suspect that you are in a relationship with a Narcissist.

1. **You are reading this book.** If you are currently holding this book in your hands and reading it that is the clearest indicator of all that you are suffering from some form of Narcissistic abuse. When I first suspected that I was being abused by someone with Narcissistic tendencies the first thing I did was some research. I dug out some therapy books, went online and chatted to other people and slowly but surely started to put the pieces together. Maybe there are several things have started happening in your relationship that just do not feel right to you. Has this person suddenly presented as very differently? Have they started telling you things that do not seem true and they want you to believe them without any evidence? Are you starting to feel a level of previously unknown self-doubt, which is causing you start to question yourself due to what this person has told you? Maybe you have even caught them out lying to you on more than one occasion. If you are in any doubt about a relationship that you are in then this is the strongest indicator

that something may not be right.

2. **They are abusive.** I know to some people this may seem like an absolute no brainer, but are they abusing you? I have often worked with people who have become very complacent around the behaviour of someone in their lives who is actually abusing them. Do they repeatedly put you down, but mask this as humour to such a degree that you know just accept it? Do you often feel like you have no say or control in your relationship with this person? Are they very good at getting you to agree to their plans as they always seem to put themselves first and never ask or require your opinion or input? If this person is emotionally, physically or otherwise abusive to you, then you are definitely in an abusive relationship. It is so important that we actually wake up to what abuse is, as one of the most common causes of abuse is emotional abuse and control. The problem is that we do not always see this as abuse, as it does not directly leave a bruise so we still tend to overlook it as abusive behaviour. Those with Narcissistic intent will often use certain manipulative tactics as you will discover in order to actually coerce you into doing those things that you do not want and make you believe that you agreed or worse, even make it seem as it was your idea. We all know deep down when we are unhappy and doing those things that we would really rather not, it becomes more harmful when we don't see that we actually do have a choice.

3. **Lack of Empathy.** Does this person lack empathy and cannot seem to understand the point of other peoples emotions? Are certain movies or songs totally lost on them? Are they confused by other people's actions when they display a caring or sensitive side? Are their words incongruent with their mood, for example, can they make an apology with no emotion behind it? Will they plea for what they want, but the intonation of their pleas sound empty and hollow? Are they childlike when they are placated, does their mood immediately go from hurt too

elated the minute they get their way, with a total disregard for the effects that it will have on you? One of the major elements of human nature that connects is with others is having and showing a strong sense of empathy. We feel for others misery and share and enjoy their sense of elation; it is one of those characteristics that warm us to others. If you are with someone who can never share others joy or pain and does not seem to care what pain they inflict on others, then this is a major warning sign.

4. **Do they also suffer with low emotional intelligence?** This is not the same as lacking in empathy, although it seems similar. A low emotional intelligence in someone can often be deduced by asking the following questions. Do they just seem to have a basic lack of understanding of other people's needs? Is the idea that someone would require help and support totally lost on them and it seems to aggravate them that another person would even require it? Do you get into lots of arguments with this person? Do they completely fail to see when you are upset with them and not give any consideration to changing their ways? Do they get upset when they are expected to understand others feelings? Is there sense of humour inappropriate and do they use offensive words at the wrong time? When you get into arguments do they always blame you and demonstrate an inability to listen to your point of view? Sometimes do they come across as just emotionally flat and totally disconnected? Do you just generally get the feeling that there is just something wrong with them? Are they prone to emotional outburst and have an inability to deal with emotional situations that are not of their own creating? Do they struggle to maintain friendships with their own family and friends and have few positive contacts? Would you say that they have strange strategies for getting what they want, instead of just asking outright for what they desire, do they attempt to gain it through bullying or coercion? Finally for this section, do they display emotional outbursts that come out of the blue and are totally inappropriate for the situation?

If you are answering yes to these questions then the person that you are currently in relationship with displays many characteristics of a Narcissist.

5. What do your true friends and family think and say? When you tell others about their behaviour do they warn you that it is not right? Have other people attempted to warn you about them in the past? Does this person attempt to segregate you from your family and friends and attempt to put you off them, by telling you things which do not seem credible or realistic? Do they put your family and friends down and attempt to turn you against them, but then make you believe that this was what you wanted. Here is a great question to ask and a clear indicator to see if you are being abused: If your best friend came to you and described your current situation and told you how this person behaved, what would your advice to them be? Think really carefully here as it is a very strong indicator of what you should be doing. Would you be telling them that the person they are with is unsuitable for them, or anyone comes to that? Would you be concerned for their safety, both physically and emotionally? Now listen to the advice that you would give to another person and take it yourself.

6. Are they addicted to the drama of any situation? Is any situation they encounter littered with sob stories, tragedy and drama? Do they earmark people out as victims, or villains and they themselves always fall into the heroic and righteous role? Do they attempt to pull everyone into these dramas to further their own cause? Do they have overblown reactions to the most normal of situations, for example overemphasising and articulating themselves when describing people and achievements? Do they become unhappy when you attempt to react in an undramatic and grown-up manner to these dramas? Will they create situations that allow them to become the rescuer? Giving them the opportunity to then recount stories time and time again where they rescued other people. In life, we often meet drama addicts and in isolation, this does not make them a Narcissist, however, when we step back and look at the big picture of this persons behaviour, we may start to build up a clearer picture of them.

7. Do they appear emotionally unbalanced? Do they suffer from dramatic shifts of self-belief and sometimes hold themselves in high regard, yet other times put themselves down? Will they outline incredible fantasies about themselves indicating that they are entitled to whatever it is that they are describing? Do they state and act in some manner that indicates they think that they are special, but at the same time have a huge crisis of confidence? They may also suffer from a victim mentality and spend a lot of time telling you just how hard done by they are in order to garner sympathy from you. A previous manager of mine would always spend more time telling me just how hard their workload was, during my own supervision. It was a clever move that would attempt to stop me from saying I was overworked and they were often successful in their attempts. Another indicator that you are with a Narcissist is being aware when they are attempting to project their insecurities onto you. This is a clear indicator of an emotionally insecure person. Do they often tell you that you could not exist without them and that you will never find another person as good as them? We can often miss these vital clues with those who have Narcissistic tendencies, as they will spend so much time chipping away at our self-esteem and forever attempting to try and bolster their own, that actually we miss how damaged they are.

8 Do they lack authenticity? Can they often present as perfect but at the same time very ingenuous, again there is that dramatic pulling in two polar opposites of their personality. They may be an attempt to present as someone very morale with a lot of humility, but their actions do anything but typify their words. You need to look closely here and judge them totally on their actions and not their words. They may talk loudly of their charitable and altruistic actions and occasionally make them, but they will demand constant and repeated validation for them. They may make bizarre and unauthentic comparisons to events and people in movies to justify themselves and almost live their life through movies. Their lack of authenticity will again pull against their other habit of displaying a lack of boundaries in many social situations.

9. **Are they psychologically damaged in some way?** They may have a history of depression or PTSD and can lapse into poor psychosis very quickly. This is not to say anyone who has suffered emotional scarring is a Narcissist, but be aware that many Narcissists have often themselves suffered emotional abuse themselves. They may fly into uncontrollable rages and become furious, but not at those things that you may expect. Their rage will often be projected at those people who they believe have received positive rewards and validation that which they believe they are entitled to. Again entitlement with Narcissists can be a key indicator, as the already damaged ego will overcompensate. For example, a previous manager of mine would always become extremely angry when they found out that any funding had gone to a rival company. The reason for this aggression was that they saw this as a direct attack upon themselves, as they were hyper-vigilant to anything that affected their self-image.

10. **They cannot be wrong or be challenged.** If you are looking for one of the clearest signs that you are with a Narcissist then try disagreeing with them or telling them "No". Now you may not have ever attempted to do this, or you may not feel that you are at that stage of development yet. But if you notice that the person who you suspect as being a Narcissist cannot handle challenges, hear the word no, or even be wrong then this again is a strong indicator of a Narcissistic personality. The reason being is that they have a very weak sense of self and again you

are looking for that personality that pulls in two separate directions at once. This time you are looking to spot that outwardly very hostile and aggressive behaviour, but inwardly very insecure and easily rattled.

Keep everything in context
By Now you are really getting an idea of the sort of characteristics and behaviours that you need to be looking out for in a person and your work and personal relationships. However, we have to keep these things within the proper context. There are many people who will display the odd one or two traits, who are not Narcissists so we have to be careful not to call them out as one. Having said that, if you are starting to build up a picture of someone and they display more than one or two of those traits then we need to start to be more cautious around them and the relationship we allow ourselves to have with them.

But remember this is only half of the story. Most people will often walk through life and wonder how and why they have repeatedly become a victim of Narcissistic abuse? Like most things in life the answer is very simple, you are easy prey. You can only be abused if you allow it and if you have stumbled from one abusive relationship to another then you give out signals and display traits that abuse people will lock onto. Now it is easy to blame, but much harder to actually take reasonability for the abuse that you have suffered. It can often be the case that our wants and desires override our good sense of what we should allow into our lives and we may even unconsciously let in and ask for this behaviour time and time again. I do not give you this advice to make you feel worse or beat you up. I want to open your eyes to this so you can see that you have the power to change things and never go back. So before we go any further, let us turn the microscope on ourselves and see if we are just screaming out to Narcissists. "Here I am, come and abuse me"

ARE YOU RIPE FOR NARCISSISTIC ABUSE?

1. Are you a people pleaser? We all like to be thought well of and help other people out and let's be honest in this world we could use more of it. We are brought up to value, others acts of kindness and are told that great people give back to the world and do for others. We are told that society values people who are selfless and benevolent and these acts are constantly upheld through all societies and media streams. So why would we not want to do good for others? I will tell you when it starts to come at great personal cost to yourself. We have become fearful of the most powerful word in the world "NO". This is not a pleasant ideology, but if you are someone who is giving, generous, always puts others first and wants to please, then sadly you are a greater and more obvious target for a Narcissist. It is good to help others when we can, but it has to be within our own physical, emotional and financial means. If you are someone who is constantly weighed down and never has any time to themselves, due to the number of activities that you constantly agree to take on, then it is time to reassess what you are doing. Why do you not feel that you can ever say "no" to another human being? Maybe you do not feel comfortable with doing this, why not? You are not obligated to always say yes to everything. We have to look at who we are and ask why we go out of our way to please others. Many times this may come down to our own self-worth and value, are we running around doing good just to get that emotional hit of others saying "Isn't' she kind", "Isn't she nice" "She is always so helpful and never says no" to anyone. If this is you, then be careful, in all my years as therapist and mediator I have never met a single person who was an over the top people pleaser and did not have self-worth issues. Needing to be the very epitome of good and kind all the time is the road to ruin, especially when a Narcissist starts to circle your waters. Do not think for one minute, that they will not take advantage of your kind people-pleasing nature and prey on your low self-worth in order to have you doing their bidding. They will take complete advantage of you and for a time you will love it, the Narcissist is actually capable of giving you that emotional hit that you crave. You are helping out another person, making them feel good, sorting out their life, even rescuing them (the biggest mistake that anyone can ever make with an abuser is thinking that they can rescue and change this person, it is never going to happen). But as your energies, self-worth, time and finances erode, they will only lean on you harder and push you further until you are completely spent. You may even find that this is the point where they leave you, in order to feed on another with greater resources. It is perfectly ok for you to have boundaries in any relationship with friends, family or at work. We all need to have boundaries and demonstrate that we don't like having them crossed. Of all the behaviours you need to examine and be aware of within yourself, it is being a people pleaser. Being kind and helpful is a great trait to have and some may even say, "it's just my nature I love to help" But be aware of what you are avoiding by living this people-pleasing lifestyle and what will it eventually cost you?

2. You need to stop being naïve and live in the real world. Just how many times does it take for you to be hit repeatedly over the head by the same person for you to stop believing that they are doing it because of the following reasons? They love you and would not do it otherwise, it is good for you and they want you to improve, or even the classic you know they don't really mean it and they have promised you it won't happen again. Or do you sell yourself the following, It is because they had a bad childhood and they did not know they were doing it. Some people will even settle for, I probably deserved it, they are not well, you asked for it and made them do it. This can lead to that most dangerous level of thought, that they just can't help themselves and I love them so I have to put up with it. One former client even told me that they sold themselves the story, It is better that they are doing it to me than someone else and If I want to be with them, then that is the way it is.

It can be very hard if you are looking for a relationship and your world if you allow it can be a lonely place. Some people will even hold the thought that being in a bad relationship is better than being on my own. The worst thought that we can ever hold as I said previously regarding a Narcissist is that "they will stop and it will get better soon and I can be the one to help them and this is the best way of doing it". Do any of these thoughts sound familiar; I could go on and fill the rest of this book with the number of excuses that I have heard from people as to why they suffer abuse and continue to suffer from it.

It is time to wake up to your own excuses as they are just keeping you living in the Narcissists warped sense of reality. Sometimes it is so hard for us to want to break free of our naivety and live in the real world, as it is much harsher than the reality that has been created for us. One of the standout movies of the last 25 years has been "The Matrix" it is an incredible movie that is so rich in metaphor and shows us how we can change our belief system. If you have never seen it, spoiler alert coming up! When Neo wakes up to his reality in this movie, it is harsh, cold, dirty and hard. The artificial world he was living in is softer, easier to navigate and kept him where he was. He did not elevate beyond his thoughts and never would have, were he not shown a way out. However, when he chose to open his eyes to those around him and himself, he changed his belief system. This is where we get the line toward the end of the movie, where Neo learns to fight back and win "He is starting to believe" You have to open your eyes and wake up to the real world. You abuser is never going to change or get better, you cannot help or save them and they only ever act out of self-interest, not because they want to help you or make you better. Start to see others and yourself with no filter. You have to start seeing the negative and that is fine. Again we are told by society to stop being negative, you are not, you are just dealing with reality, become a realist. Be aware of those who keep telling you not to be suspicious of others actions, it is perfectly ok. Stop romanticising, glamorising, or even over analysing your Narcissist abuser. These delusional filters that "you choose" to place over abusing behaviour just give the Narcissist complete free reign to go on abusing you with your blessing. Any type of abuse, no matter what excuses are made "Is Not OK"

3. Do you have a desire to be liked and need validation? Be really honest is this you? Of course, it is, because actually, it is most of us. We all love to think that we are liked, loved and cannot but help feel a sense of pride when we receive positive attention for the work that we do, or through our thoughts or actions. We have even created platforms for ourselves to measure are popularity and feedback, checked your Facebook page recently to see who has liked your last post, picture or status? We all like to think that we are doing well in life and for many of us this will come from what we hear and see from others. Now while there are certain arenas where this is acceptable, such as work placed supervision or genuine compliments, however, we have to keep our need and desire for validation in check. If your desire is to be liked, loved and wanting others attention it will put you on the very dangerous ground as it will cause you to change your actions, opinions and thoughts to agree with others just for appearances sake. So ask yourself, just how easy is it for a Narcissist to control and abuse you if you are overly concerned by how the world sees you? If someone can get you to change your opinion, thoughts, beliefs and act in a manner that you would not normally, by feeding you the idea that if you do, as they say, it will make you look amazing to others. Then you will willingly follow and comply with their actions.

4. Are you a drama addict yourself? For many people, the lure of some drama in their lives is too much to resist and a Narcissist will be only too happy to provide you with this. We all like a break from the mundane and we can often be drawn to those people who pull us in with shock revelations and exciting tales of themselves and others. If you are someone who can be easily drawn into this web then you are easy prey for the Narcissist and they feed you drama after drama and press all of your emotional buttons. Just be aware if you are someone who seeks and looks for drama in life or are easily drawn into others drama for some excitement. You may well be making up one half of a partnership that a Narcissist craves.

5. Do you suffer with low self-esteem or a poor sense of self? So many of us can walk through life and never really feel that we have a good sense of who we are and where we are going. We may often feel that we are just drifting from one thing to another and struggling to find our way and purpose. Now, this may apply to many people and generally, we never give enough consideration to our purpose and plan. However, it can become harmful if we realise that we fail to progress and move forward in life, due to never feeling good enough to achieve our own goals or dreams. We may strongly lack a good sense of our self-worth and rely on others to make you feel good or tell you where you should be going. Just how attractive are you to someone who wishes to manipulate you, if you constantly feel uncertain of who you are and are questioning your own actions? Remember if you do not have a strong plan for yourself, someone else will. This poor sense of self may also cause you to spend too much time fantasising about your life and not being grounded in reality. Remember the Narcissist's personality will cater to your fantasy`s and attempt to distort your reality by promising you your heart's desire. It is far better to remain grounded and living a life less colourful rather than have the Narcissist paint you a false picture of a life that will never happen.

6. Are you emotionally dependent? When we discuss emotional dependence we often assume that our levels of dependence are attached to people, but this is not always the case. We can often become emotionally dependent on outcomes of various situations and this can lead to all sorts of dependency problems. Dependency within itself can just be a problem; obviously, we are dependent on certain things in life, water, air, food and won't get too far without them. However, when we have those basic needs met, we can then often turn to having our emotional needs met. For example, we have emotional needs, our need for love, affection, happiness etc. These all give us emotional certainty and when we get them we feel good about ourselves and this fulfils a need within our ego. It is when we don't get these emotional hits and start attaching our desire to feel good to events and people that we become vulnerable to abuse. Now think of it this way, if you were totally emotionally secure in every way and felt no need or desire to be with anyone other than yourself, it would be much harder for someone to abuse you in a relationship. If you were totally 100 percent secure and happy to be on your own and had a state of total reliance, as soon as someone started to abuse you, you would think "I don't need this, I am better off on my own" and you would get rid of them. But let us be honest not everyone is that mentally strong and it is worth pointing out that mental toughness is just a state of mind that can be developed. So start to ask yourself some of the following questions to see if this applies to you.   Are you just happy to be on your own? Now answer this honestly, most people will say they are, but they are not. I mean are you really happy to be on your own, even over your birthday and Christmas day!! It is not an easy thought, is it? Many of us want to attach to another person for all the right reasons and again this is a good thing, but it is when we feel we are dependent on others for our emotional happiness that we become vulnerable.

7. Are you excessively contentious? Are you someone who gives more value to others and allow your own opinions to be devalued? Will you often make your opinion easy to dismiss and even devalue it yourself? The great thing to remember about opinions is that we should not mistake them for facts, so yours are as valuable as the next persons. Always be aware of those people who will tell you there opinion is a fact and under-value yours. Have you got an avoidant personality type? Do you back away quickly from certain discussions and not join in? Do you often self-isolate? These are clear signs that you are scared to put yourself out there as you may well fear the outcome of the discussion or situation. Do you over intellectualize some-one else's behaviour in order to justify them doing something wrong? This is actually one of the worst things you can ever do around an abusive person, as when you do you are just handing them the stick to beat you with time and time again and saying "no its Ok, you can hit me with it I understand that you need to do it" There is no acceptable rationale for this type of behaviour, ever. It does not matter, whatever story you're told about your abusers background, harsh childhood, mental health, if you are over intellectualising it in any way, you are wrong. Do not let any ever tell you different. Unless someone is so ill that they cannot recognise right from wrong, then there is never a reason for them to be abusing you. I had a former boss who`s behaviour was so appalling it was unbelievable. I could also not believe the excuses that everyone, including their boss, made for them. One person actually said to me one day "They are a complete Narcissist and totally abusive, I hate them, they push their boundaries with me all the time" I asked them why they felt the behaviour was acceptable. They replied "Well they do a lot of good work for the company, spend a lot of hours here and really care about the job" Talk about justifying the Narcissistic abuse.

8 Are you addicted to approval seeking behaviour? Is the out-come to you so important that you would sacrifice anything to get that all-important pat on the head? I once dated some-one who within the first few weeks was constantly validating me for absolutely everything I did and use to tell me that "No man had ever done that for her before" How good did I feel? But then as quickly as it started it stopped. My first thoughts were, is something wrong. Not getting those "Your amazing texts any more"? But quite quickly I realised that they wanted me to up my game to receive my reward, the things that were required of me to get my emotional hit required greater time and financial sacrifice. As you can imagine as soon as I realised this I ended the relationship as they may well not have been the well-balanced life partner that I saw myself with. Through this, I also learnt to not become attached to the outcome and would only do things for genuine reasons and not for reward.

9. Do you still possess great levels of immaturity? When we are young we are taught that good behaviour brings good outcomes and when we do behave and get that outcome we have living proof that the story we have just been told is true. The problem is with Narcissistic people, they will attempt to keep us in this childlike state in order to have us emotionally attached to outcomes. We behave like children and get really upset when we don't get what we were promised and will then do anything to redress the balance. If you still get these strong emotional urges to be rewarded then it is time to step away from the child`s table and sit with the grownups.

By now you really have a solid basis of information regarding those people in your life who you suspect as being abusive and also if you are someone who is an easy target for abusive behaviour. Now before we move on to what you need to do about it, let us first look a little at why Narcissists have it so easy in life.

WHY THEY DO WHAT THEY DO AND WE LET THEM GET AWAY WITH IT

The answer to this is easy, bad programming and the pressures that society places on decency, honesty and having good morals. As we have already discovered having great morels and high standards is a great way to lead your life, just a pity that Narcissists have a different playbook from yours. Basically, our society has what are known as Norms (Be honest, nice, kind and decent and all good things will come to you). We can pick this up from religious text, parents, school, films, TV, social media, just about anywhere you go. Society basically just teaches us to behave and be good to other people. As I have said on the whole this is a great way to live your life and brilliant if everyone stuck to these rules. The problem is this type of thinking does not prepare you for an abusive relationship or dealing with a Narcissist. I told you this was going to be a tough read and one that breaks from the conventions of usual thinking. Believe it or not, there are some people who are so bound to conventions in life that they actually develop a fear of displeasing others (Emotophobia). Now the problem is when we have a Narcissist enter our lives they will always attempt to sell themselves on the good virtues they bestow. I have never yet encountered one Narcissist, who did not go to great lengths to let me know how morale, decent and upright they were. One even said to me "I would never, ever do anything to hurt you, ask all my friends they will all tell you I am really honest, loyal and total decent" Well after they had two affairs and ruined numerous lives, their only response was to cling on to the false belief that they were still really decent and did not deserve the negative fallout they got from others due to their own actions. This was textbook Narcissism, as they were totally unable to face the reality of what they did and who they were.

Yes, the Narcissist will enter your camp as the classic wolf in sheep's clothing and if they spot that you have any kind of hang up or issues, they will target you and then their game begins. Remember these people can smell a lack of assertiveness and self-esteem a mile away and will test you by going against societies norms of decency to see if you stand up to them and if you don't they know that you can be abused. The trouble is with many people, is that we will often make excuses for this bad behaviour especially in the UK, where if someone pushes to the front of the queue we are more likely to just tut and quietly mumble "really did you see that". We will then most likely justify the behaviour to make it fit into a social norm. "Oh well they did have a lot of shopping" or "Well they were old" or we may even attempt to justify bad behaviour by thinking of times when we have been less than saintly and say "Well I would have done the same if I was in their position" Some of you may even secretly admire them for their poor behaviour in the same way that we admire those who are bold enough to go for what we want in life and just grab it and take it. This is actually one of the main causes of why Narcissists are rewarded constantly for their behaviour and will never ever change. It works for them to display this behaviour and they are more than often rewarded for it and sometimes looked up to and admired for it. They actually see that there is no downside to their behaviour and sometimes have very little or no conscience, so what do they have to lose, nothing"

One of our other reasons you may have for putting Narcissists on this higher level is for the protection of your own EGO. That way when we are deceived by them, we can say something like, "Ah yes but they are an evil genius and a huge intellectual, and no one could defeat them" This way we will not feel bad for being deceived. Well, I have news for you; they are not evil geniuses who have been genetically altered in a secret government laboratory they are people just like you and I, but they choose not to follow the rules of society. So to gain further insight, let us take a look at the world of the Narcissist, from inside their head.

WELCOME TO THE MIND OF A NARCISSIST

For a moment and I am not suggesting that you live like this at all, but just for a moment, I want you to imagine this was your strategy in life for getting what you want. First imagine something you desire, no matter what it is, be it a physical item, a favour from someone, forcing someone to behave in a certain way, anything at all. Now just imagine that in order to get it, you will do pretty much anything you desire and know that you can get away with it, order to obtain it and it won't bother you in the slightest what damage or harm you cause to others. You can behave as badly as you like as long as you get what you want. If you get caught, you know that it does not really matter, as that is just part of life and the game and well, you know people get over things and of course you can just explain it all away by saying something like "well you know what I'm like when I want something I just have to go after it" You could even think ahead and actually think of a good reason for your bad behaviour, maybe making it look like you "bent the rules a little" so others would benefit, yes that will do it, always a good excuse "I Only did it for the good of, the company, our relationship, your development, whatever suits. People are always willing to let those who are doing good get away with stuff. So now you can go ahead and, shout, bully, lie, manipulate, intimidate and hurt as many people as much as you like to get what you want. Oh and remember to make sure that you make it looks like you are the victim if anyone calls you out on your behaviour. If you upset someone for shouting remember, "It's because you are stressed and overworked and do more hours than anyone else in the whole company". If you are caught having an affair with a married man, "You could not help it as you were vulnerable and did not know what you were doing". Remember if you do get caught this is a great time to admit to weaknesses and flaws in your character and you can make up something about a history of abuse, people love that sort of thing and it always makes them want to take care of you. If you can also cry at this point and actually make someone else look or feel bad for having caught you out then all the better, anything to keep them off the scent and from looking at the hurt and damage that you have just caused. However at this time remember to still keep your goals in mind, as this is just a temporary delay to getting what you want. The other thing to also bear in mind is that most people are just too scared to challenge this sort of behaviour and if you talk loud and aggressive enough for long enough, they will most likely give in. The reason that you can get away with this behaviour is that most people just want things to return to normal and for the pain to go away and it all be comfortable again. So you have all the power and you can bring pain to their world, then when they do what you want, stop shouting and make the pain go away for them, but only when you get what you want, you are also hugely aware that most people will make excuses for you and use the reasons that you give others to justify your behaviour. Some will even admire this as you know really they want to be just like you.   There how was that little roller coaster ride for you? Now you can see just how and why a Narcissist will never change their behaviour and just why they get away with it time and time again, until now!

Let me ask you a question and be really honest with yourself, as if you are not it's only you who you are lying to. After what you have already read and learnt, do you now honestly really believe that the abuse is going to just stop and things, will just get better without you doing anything at all? I really hope that your answer is "No" if it is not, then it should be. By now you should be building up an idea of what makes up the Narcissistic mind and why your only option here is to take action. The first self-help book I ever read suggested that if you are unhappy with something in your life and never do anything thing about it, then you're like a whining dog with a thorn in its paw. You complain about it daily to everyone and say how bad it is, but you never do anything about it. The book suggested that you have one of three options. Your first option is that you can carry on and put up with it until it destroys you. Or the second option is that you can attempt to change the situation; in this case, we are looking to either change the other person or relationship. Now if you are in any kind of Narcissistic relationship I really would not bother with this option, as they will never change, despite what they may tell you. Going with this option you really have to be looking to change the relationship. Or the third option and the one that will start to yield the best results is that you need to change yourself. Now the good news is that reading this book will help you to start making some of those changes to your life. So you have options and choices in life, always remember that, even when you don't think you have choices, you do. Remembering that you have options and choices in life can be one of the most powerful thoughts you can take on board. As the more options you realise you have, the more powerful you become. Now it is time to start making those first steps forward and making those powerful changes to your life.

2. BREAKING AWAY FROM NARCISSISTIC ABUSE

Step one to breaking free, go back to you.

L et me ask you another question and it will be one that you have not considered in a while. What are your goals, dreams and desires for yourself? Not for anyone else but for you, do you want to travel, lose weight, leave your job, get a new job, get a promotion, take up a new hobby or learn an instrument? Whatever they are, when was the last time that you did something for yourself? Now a lot of people will go straight away for, well I want this for that person and I want my children, sister or parents to be happy. There is a really good reason for asking yourself what you and you alone want. It is all well and good wanting good things for those around you, but look at what you are doing, when you do this, you are being over-generous and starting to lose sight of who you are and what you want. So now really think about what you want in life and also the reasons why you alone want them, just you only you! Now think about the barriers that prevent you from having them, be honest with yourself. Ask yourself why these barriers are barriers, for what reason do they prevent you from achieving what you want. At this stage, you may be identifying all manner of barriers in your life and starting to ask why they are there at all. You may even realise that there is a person or people in your life that are actively stopping you from achieving your goals. If this is the case, ask yourself for what reason do they not want you to have this? You really need to think hard about this last question and there is a good reason why someone abusive will want to stop you from achieving your goals. If you are in any kind of abusive relationship with a Narcissist, the questions that I have just asked you are the things a Narcissist never want you to think about. When was the last time they asked you want you and you alone wanted and why? This is where you need to start living in your mind, you need to start finding who you are again and looking at what you most desire. It is your first step to start actively breaking free of Narcissistic abuse. The number of times I can recall losing sight of my goals and dreams as the person who I was in a relationship with knew that one of the main secrets to controlling me was to tell me that "what I wanted was impossible". I remember sharing a dream of wanting to become a public speaker and it was completely trashed by my partner at the time who told me it was impossible, I needed to hold all manner of qualifications that I had never heard of and that I lacked any experience in this field. This was a repeated pattern and it happened again when I wanted to move my therapeutic world into a corporate field, I was told that no one would ever come to see me, for I was "Not successful in business". I was also sold by them the idea that they only did this for "my own best interests", as they wanted the best for me and "did not want me to look foolish". They never once offered solutions and only ever put up barrier after, barrier. Interestingly enough I have gone on, to work very successfully in both these fields and never did obtain that qualification they spoke of.

So why is it important that if you want to break free of an abusive relationship that you start pursuing your dreams and desires. Well for a start it will highlight who those people are who wish to keep you contained and do not want yo,u breaking out and becoming too confident. Remember the Narcissist will not want this to happen to you, for their greatest fear will be you breaking away from their abuse until they are done with you. Secondly, if you start to refocus your mind in a new direction (your goals and dream) you will start to remember just who you are again and no longer be the pale imitation of a person that a Narcissist wishes you to be. We can all lose ourselves within a relationship a little and we will enjoy the feeling of merging with others, it is part of why we look to connect with another. When we do this we sometimes take on part of the other people's characteristics and language patterns and even end up liking new things and freely giving up things that we find of no use any more. This merging and connection is fertile ground for the Narcissist and they will use it to grow and reshape you into the form that they wish. But this version of you will be a version without confidence, focus or self-esteem. So imagine if someone who was in an abusive relationship started to meet and talk with other people who had broken away from and left an abusive relationship. What positive effects would that have on you? This is man reason why a Narcissist will want to have complete control over a person's movements, they fear them having contact with others who will open their eyes to the abuse and empower them.

Step two to breaking free, reach out and believe.

There are those people in your world who are sitting watching and waiting. They genuinely love you, care for you and have to sit and watch what you are going through every day. They are waiting for the day when you finally approach them with your fears, suspicions about the abuse that you are suffering. They will welcome you in, listen, help and offer good advice and maybe even salvation and shelter. They are called your family and real friends. If you go and speak to them and ask them their thoughts on your life, work and relationships and ask them to be really honest, you will be surprised at what they will tell you. Ask them what they really think of those people in your life you suspect as abusing you. But this time do it with a new mindset. A mindset that is open, willing to listen and believe what is being said. When you demonstrate that you can do this, those genuine loved ones will listen and open up and tell you what they have been holding onto for months maybe years. If you are going to break free of being a victim of Narcissistic abuse you need to speak out, listen openly and be willing to believe the thoughts of others. Just be mindful to choose wisely those who you confide in. This simple step may be hard but is essential to helping you build up a clear picture and seeing the other side of what is going on within your world. The important part here is that you are open and believe what is being said to you. So many people are advised and warned that they are stuck in abusive relationships; however, they will just hear the words and dismiss them, as they challenge the world that the Narcissist has built around you. Allow their words to start bringing this world down. Let the truth they have been longing to tell you, bring focus and clarity back into your world.

Step three to breaking free, taking back control of your thoughts and building up your energies.

You are where you are at any one time within your life due in part to your beliefs. Those who believe they can achieve great things will always stand a much greater chance of achieving them. Your world is built on beliefs and the one thing that Narcissists excel in are distorting your world and building this world of false beliefs for you to live in. It's a small world and you're safely contained and cannot move too far from it. They will feed you the beliefs that they need you to hold to keep you where they need you and they do it incredibly well. But here is the thing, if you choose to just take a look over and around the walls that they have built you will start to see that although the walls may look very high and appears to be thick, strong and made of solid material. If you actually looking at these walls from a different angle they are actually paper thin and you can tear them down.

By now from what you may have already learnt there are those people within your life who will tell you a great many things in an attempt to control you with nothing more than lies. Or to break lies down more clearly, reality-distorting beliefs that will feed into any negative thoughts or feelings that you hold around yourself. It is time to go back now and really start to examine who you were before you met those who gave you these beliefs.

There is something that I talk to many of my clients about and I like to remind them of on their first session with me and that is getting back to their sense of self-worth and in order to do this, I take them back to a time long ago. When you were born, you were not born with anything issues, problems, neurosis psycho-logical fears, phobias or feelings of low self-worth. It is almost as if you were born this perfect gem. But over the years people who you met dumped their own psychological rubbish on you, gave you false beliefs and generally distorted your self-esteem. Now in order to deal with all of these distortions, you may have attempted to paper over this rubbish in order to hide it from the world. However as much as you pretend that other people's rubbish and beliefs that have been dumped upon you are not there, they are. Now it is time to deal with your negative feel-ings regarding who you are. So you need to reach in, wipe all the rubbish off of that perfect gem you were born to be and start liv-ing without it.

 When I remind people that actually many of the things that happened to them in life were not their fault, bad luck or how they were made or born, many of them immediately start to feel better about who they are. The second and very important thing that I help people to realise is that in order to selfheal, you have to accept that you can control very few things in this world especially other people. You really cannot ever control other people unless they choose to let you. You have only ever been controlled yourself as you have allowed yourself to be controlled.

In actual fact, there are only two things that you can completely control. The first and most important thing you can control are the thoughts in your head. The only other thing you can ever control is how you wish to feel about and react to any situation that ever happens to you. These two things together make up the only true power that exists within the world, the power to act on your own thoughts. I will say that again as it is vital to your breaking free and recovering from any kind of abuse. "The thoughts in your head and how you wish to feel about and react to any situation that ever happens to you are the only real power that exists in life". Now really think about this as it is something that narcissists all around the world will tell you is just not true and will have spent most of their lives convincing you of just the opposite. You can choose your own thoughts, how you wish to feel and choose how to react to any situation you are presented with. You really can, you have just not realised it or forgot to remember it. This is a thought that is actually very easy to forget and a basic human right. If you only take one thing away from this book that you hold onto and put it into action, then make sure this is it.

But it is so easy to forget that you have this power, as within our everyday life we can often forget the true power of our own thoughts and freedom to choose. We will allow ourselves to be carried away with other's politics, thoughts, viewpoints and beliefs. So it is no wonder when someone with a strong Narcissistic intent comes into our lives that we are easily controlled.

So now we have accepted our new found power, how do we use it every day to make positive changes? Well, the good news is you have already started. Just realising and remembering that it is you who are in control of that voice in your head and what you want to do is the first step.

The next step towards using your power does take some practise, but practising it is very simple, you just need to become better at actually remembering you have it. The reason we forget that we have a choice with how we can emotionally react is that it is so very easy to take this power away from people. You have already discovered how effective distortion is and how others can create fantasy worlds to contain us in. You have also seen how others can make you forget who you are and create false beliefs that make you act in a way that pleases them. So look on this as you wake up call and now you have been reminded of this power, it is time to take the next vital step forward.

Remembering To Remember Your One True Power

As a therapist, many people come and see me for all manner of issues and I'm always able to help them see where they can make changes to improve all areas of their lives. I always make it a point of ending my sessions by telling those who come to see me, "You can have what you want, (Your goals and dreams) as long as you remember to do whatever it is you need to do to make them real and do not give your power away" and I say this for one good reason. I would go so far as to say the only time people fail to get the outcomes they want is when they forget or are manipulated to forget their one true power. "You are in control of the thoughts in your head and you can choose how you wish to feel and react to any given situation". Say it to yourself right now. "I am in control of the thoughts in my head and I can choose how I wish to feel and react to any given situation". It feels good to remember this and say it doesn't it? Now say it again and when you do remember those times when you used this power and it felt good. Remember when you exerted control over an area of your own life and how good it felt when you made a decision based on what you wanted. It is so important that you start to access these thoughts and memories as they are your strongest reminders of how your true power works.

One of the most important parts of remembering and using your power of individual thought is to ensure that you have the energy to exert it. One of the main reasons that those people who I work with fail to remember to use this great power is tiredness! If you are not taking care of yourself physically and emotionally then you will feel tired and drained and you will be easier to control and manipulate. Now if you have someone in your life who is a constant and emotional drain upon you, then they are going to leave you tired and exhausted. Being around Narcissistic people or someone who you constantly have to do battle with can take some energy and you may never have thought that this was a relevant part of your existence, until now!

It was only when I finally confronted a true narcissist with everything they had done to me and other people and I had them bang to rights that I found out the power of taking back my own thoughts and energies. I had all the evidence against them and they knew the game was up and there was no more game playing, gas lighting, manipulating me and they did the only thing they could do and that was flee. They were absolutely done for and had no more ammunition or tricks. They knew that I would never trust them again, so there was nothing left to be had, they could not prey on me anymore. They went into full flight, of course, they had to attempt to make that last play and told me that it was actually my fault they had done all these horrendous things to people. But by then, I was bullet-proof to their abuse. I have never felt so happy, relaxed and empowered and it was a turning point in my life. I was only able to do this by remembering that I had a choice in how I could react to their words and their manipulations. I conserved my energies and took back my power just by remembering that I had a right to my own thoughts and ideas. I had forgotten this simple fact that robbed me of my power. Just imagine what it is like to be denied your thoughts and ideas and made to believe that you cannot do certain things, after a while, you start to believe the reality distortions. If this is the world that you are living in, start rehearsing to yourself, every day your new mantra. "I am in control of the thoughts in my head and I can choose how I wish to feel and react to any given situation".

As soon as I did this, I felt this rush of euphoria and started to regain all of my emotional energies.

Step 4 to breaking free, get to know your fears and find confidence

How am I going to survive and live without this person in my life I thought? I cannot possibly manage to complete all of the things on my own. I knew that I had a good brain and was capable of accomplishing a great many things. In my past, I had held managerial positions, closed deals for over a million pounds and was a respected therapist, so why did I have this terrible fear that if I was ever on my own I would not be able to cope. The answer was simple because I had allowed my fears to take over my world and control my actions.

Would you like to know what a fear is? Quite simply put a fear is nothing more than us thinking about and putting our focus on something that has not or may never happen. There you go that is it, that is what a fear is; when you spend time thinking about something bad that may not ever happen. All of our fears are pure imagination, how many times have you focused on a fear only to never ever have it manifest itself within your life? The problem is we do and we breathe life into our fears and live them time and time again within our mind until we start acting as if they are real and then limit our actions to fit in with them. Now while we all have fears in our life we will often confuse them with real danger. Danger is something that exists in the world. You don't just cross a busy road with your eyes closed and tell yourself that your fear of being run over is in your head do you. No, you are aware that the danger is clear and present and would not do anything to put yourself in its way. But we can often mix the two up and our fears are a fertile breeding ground for narcissistic abuse. Let us jump back for the moment into the mind of the Narcissist (not a great place to live, but I promise you it will help you to break free from their abuse). So within the mind of the Narcissist, there is a self-preservation element that says they have to survive at all costs. Now when I mean all costs I do mean ALL costs and as I have stated any line will be crossed to achieve their goals. So when you as the trusting individual share a fear or a concern with a narcissist they just think "Brilliant, I will store that one away until I need it" it is great ammunition for them. The advantage that Narcissists have is our encouragement from all areas of our world to share our secrets. Modern day society has taught us to share and be trusting of everyone. We tell our most intimate secrets over social media. We are used to seeing mainstream programs where people let cameras film, them 24/7. People open up to millions of people over the internet. We have been taught that it is great to share. A trouble shared is a trouble halved I often hear. As a therapist, I encourage people to explore the deepest and innermost recesses of their mind to help them achieve change. So it is only natural that you will share your concerns and fears with people. But what happens when that person is a Narcissist? They now hold a huge piece of the puzzle in their hands to what makes you tick and how to control you and your actions. I was once unfortunate enough to confess to a Narcissistic manager my concerns over the ability to connect to the other members of the team. They promptly used my concern to divide me from other members of the team and then they would often tell me in supervisions that the team did not connect with me. I was lucky in this case as the manager left and the house of cards they built fell apart very quickly and we realised what they had been doing to members of the team. Now sharing is a part of life and we all need to offload and talk to others. However please take this next piece of advice seriously. Stop sharing all of your information with everyone you meet and on social platforms. Knowledge is power and knowledge of your fears and concerns to a Narcissist is absolute power. Choose who you talk to wisely, make sure that the person who you wish to confide in is not ticking all of the boxes for a card-carrying Narcissist. I have known Narcissists be able to manipulate people into staying in a long term abusive relationship, just because they have opened up shared a concern about being on their own. You are handing someone one of your greatest assets and treasures when you do this and they will just take it and beat you over the head with it. Keep wise counsel and keep your fears private unless you are really certain you can trust someone. It is often the case that Narcissistic people will be the ones who want to fish for your concerns and this is very relevant to those who you have just met and want to know all about you.

It is far better that you get a grip on the reality of your life and your fears and concerns before you start opening up and sharing them with anyone and everyone. So how do we do this? Well, one way to do this is to start to become more centred and focused on the reality of our lives. Making sure that we are not catastrophizing a situation and staying rooted in reality can be a good step in the right direction. Always ask yourself, Is your fear based on reality or something that you are just choosing to tell yourself? Poke your fear with a few sticks to see if it stands up to some testing. For example, if you have a fear of being alone and are desperately clinging to a relationship instead of focusing your thoughts on the fear for example "what if they leave me? "I'll never find another one like them" "I am too old no one else will want me". Try asking yourself a better quality of question and notice what answers come out of your mind. For example "Are their other people my age that are single who would treat me better?" "Where can I go to find them" "What is great about not having that abusive relationship anymore?" "How much fun will I have dating and meeting, new people?" Now just notice what this does to your mind. It is called reframing the situation and a great way of focusing your unreal fears.

Also, start to become aware of these fears and concerns are

being reinforced by anyone? It always serves Narcissistic people to constantly remind you of your fears and "loneliness, being unloved, unemployed, homeless or being without your loved ones" Notice the elements that they are labelling in your life in order to keep you contained. For example, do you have a partner who says "Well no one else would want you at your age" and then makes out it is a joke? We can easily take on board others unkind comments both consciously and unconsciously and soon find that all of those digs and "jokes" have started to have a very negative effect on our existence. I used to work for a Narcissistic manager who would "jokingly" insult their staff telling them how bad they all were at their jobs and none of them worked as well or as hard as they did. Now it was hardly the gold standard of motivational speeches and you may have experienced other people within positions of power doing the same. However, the fears that these tirades brought up in other members of staff was quite powerful and they would often end up stressed and anxious feeling like they were trapped in a job that they could not do. The work teams fears and concerns of being ineffectual at work were preyed upon by a Narcissist who lorded their heightened sense of self-worth and apparent success over them on a daily bases. It is important that you start to become mindful to see through the words that impact upon you and notice the effect that they are having on your emotions. Also as ever question the reality of what you are being told, time and time again.

You will always find that anyone who generally puts others down as a norm through humour or insults or lies is attempting to mask their own poor self-worth. I have often noticed that one of the personality traits of people with abusive intent could be summarised as "If you cannot build your own tower very high, then knock everyone else`s tower down around you". If you do that then you can forget about your own low self-worth and keep the attention off of you. For many years I knew someone who would have to constantly make veiled humorous attacks on anyone and everyone as they had terrible low self-esteem. The person was quite overweight and had a number of issues, but instead of concentrating on dealing with those, would just make sure that they kept on rolling out the insults. However, with Narcissists, it is sometimes more calculated and thought through. Many Narcissists will hold the belief that attack is the best form of securing and ensuring that their own needs are met. After all, if you can keep someone down by chipping away at their confidence levels they are so much easier to control.

Step 5 to breaking free, emotionally detaching from an abusive person

So why when we know that something or someone will keep on hurting us do we keep going back and sticking our hand in the fire, hoping that the next time it won't hurt so badly. We just blindly listen to and believe their lies that "it really was the last time and it won`t happen again". The problem is that we just want and hope to believe that it could be different and that it will be ok? To be honest the reasons are numerous and we may fear that old terrible enemy, change!!! Of all of the fears that live in the world, change is the greatest and can keep us where we are. Now we will often override this by making our reality in our heads not as bad as it is. Yes, it hurts to be putting up with this abuse, but maybe it is not that bad and it could be worse. Well, this is your way of making sure you avoid change and to be honest you know this and so does your abuser.

The only way to really fully now make sure that you are totally detached from this person is by fully emotionally detaching from them. When you do this you will finally be able to feel that true sense of freedom and see the Narcissist within your life for who they really are. When any of my clients have made that decision that they finally want to be free of an abuser or at the very least remove all emotional attachment from them, so they feel stronger and more centred I will take them through the following technique.

Please be aware that this technique can be very difficult to undertake unless you are really sure that you are in the correct emotional place to move forward. You also need to follow it very carefully. It is such a powerful technique as it uses visualisations and the power of your mind to totally disassociate from those people within your life who have abused and hurt you. As it is such a powerful technique, you may wish to have a friend sit with you to do this, as it does involve going over past hurts in order to purge them and diminish them. You may also want to write certain sections of this therapeutic technique down as you go. You can also repeat it more than once if you feel the need to.

Detaching from an emotionally abusive person technique

First, you need to picture your abuser and take yourself back to a time when they hurt you, emotionally, physically or financially. Go over one of the times that they hurt you. See it as if it were happening to you in your head. Now almost as if you had a remote control. Pause your thoughts and freeze the image you have in your head.

Now change the picture so that you are not in it any more, as if you are seeing it happening to someone else. Move the picture further away and as you do just focus on the face of the abuser. Now put a label on this image you have of them, for example, you may call this first image, Bully, Narcissistic abuser or whatever comes to mind. Make sure you choose a label that reflects reality and not one that excuses them of the behaviour. Now store this first image of your abuser in your head under the new label you have just created.

Now repeat the process again and choose another time this

person hurt you. Again choose a time you remember well and visualise it as if it were happening to you. Now experience some pain, but then pause the image and move it away as if it were happening to someone else, (totally detach from the image) as if you were just watching it. Now focus on your abuser and again give them a label that reflects this behaviour, emotional abuser, manipulator etc. Do not give them a label that excuses or justifies the behaviour. Now store this second image of your abuser in your head under its new label.

Now repeat this process as many times as you feel necessary, normally 5 to six times is enough and then go on to the next stage.

One by one I want you to bring back all of the images and say the label that you gave them either out loud or in your head. Bring back each image time and time again and keep saying the labels to yourself or out loud.

Keep letting the images circulate and keep saying the labels until you really feel any emotional control this person once had on you completely disappearing. Just keep the images flash up in front of you with the labels in front of them.

The final stage is to bring up all of the images together in a college. Sit them all along-side each other until you can see them all and say all of the labels out loud or in your head.

Now however you wish start to get rid of these images one by one in your head. Move them away until they disappear, fade them out, see them going up in flames and as you do see you're past associations and relationship with this abusive person also go the same way

Now relax and see yourself in your new life, away from the influence of this person and from under their control and manipulation. See how happy you are and how free that you feel.
Let it go now, it is time to move on and heal yourself.

3. HEALING FROM NARCISSISTIC ABUSE

What makes healing from Narcissistic about so hard?

The main problem with those who have been involved within a Narcissist is the desire to keep going back and returning for more of the same. For some people, Narcissists are a fascination and their behaviour is almost drug-like. We have to be prepared to extract ourselves totally from those people who constantly hurt us, so we can take time to heal, grow strong and become the person we need to. Narcissists have the ability to bring all of those wounds of yours out into the open, they make you consciously aware of your wounds time and time again. Remember they do not want you to heal, as an open wound to a Narcissist is that area where they will feed from time and time again, until you are emotionally, mentally and financially drained. The narcissist in your life may have even come to you in the form of a healer or guide, be aware most Narcissist will have the ability to change shape to please your needs. I have had people within workplaces pose as mentors who have declared they were there to help and support me, only to work behind my back to destabilise my work and efforts and attempt to remove me from my work placed position. They are not your healer or guide and will not take away your pain, only you can empower yourself to do this. You have to have the ability to cut yourself off from these people and when you have found the strength to, it is time to block all access to and from them and start to heal. No matter how tempted you are to return, you will never be rewarded for your efforts and as much as you are thinking about them, I guarantee you they are not thinking about you.

Ask a better question and get a better answer

We often say that time can be a great healer and for some people this is true, but for others, it is nothing more than words that they hear. The concern with time healing us is that for some people they just run those poor strategies time and time again within their heads and totally relive the moments of abuse and harm. Some people may even get into the age-old internal question of "why did this happen to me" or "Why are they like this, what do they get out of it" or the absolute classic "I would not do that to another person, so why would they do it to me" Well I think by now I have covered in depth why Narcissists behave this way, but for now let us just remember this. You will never change them or heal yourself with constant "why" questions and it will just drive you deeper and deeper into the abuse. The simple truth is, these things have happened to you and while understanding of a situation can be interesting to know why even if you ever got that answer it would not help you to heal. It is far better to know that you have extracted yourself from the relationship and you can you start by asking a better quality of question. When I finally confronted and ejected a narcissist from my life, I realised that if they wanted to, they could have easily crawled back into my world and did attempt to several times. I knew that the only way that I could ever be free of them, was to start seeing myself as someone who did not need them. So I simply started to ask myself positive and healing questions such as, "*What are the good things about my life now that this person has gone*", the answer came back very quickly and I started to realise the total freedom that I possessed within my world now. It was still painful, but I was able to start to take ownership of myself, my problems and the world I was living in. Once I got into the habit of asking better questions I started to ask what I was really interested in and what would make me feel better about myself. The answer again came back very quickly and for the first time in my life, I discovered meditation. I had been a therapist for many years and always been aware of the power of the mind and using the subconscious, but I had never used it to learn to just sit and be. Using this really positive and powerful tool started to become the bases for my own self-healing and every day I would ask myself questions like *"what it is that I would want from my world and how I would like to be"* Now I will say at this stage this did not solve all of my emotional concerns at this time, but it really gave me the direction to move to the next step, learning to just be happy.

Just sit and be

Now anyone who has ever been to one of my talks or knows me will know that I am very fond of quoting Blaise Pascal's famous quote and as I have said earlier in this book, "All of humanity's problems stem from man's inability to sit quietly in a room alone". This is fundamentally the most important skill and mindset you can ever achieve and desire if you are to ever break free and heal yourself from abuse. Just put yourself in this mindset for a minute and see how you would feel if you were this person.

I would happily say that I am very happy with myself, I like the way I look. I know I am not everyone's cup of tea, but I think I look ok. I am generally just as happy with my own company as I am with other people. I like to go and socialise, but I also love being at home with a boxset or a great book. I hold no negative thoughts around myself, who I am or what I do. I am certain that good things will come into my world as and when I make them. I know that I am secure and comfortable with myself and would not allow my feelings to take over and put me in a place or with a person that made me feel uncomfortable. I really value myself and do not need validation from others, but appreciate genuine compliments. My friends would say I am very calm and rock-like. I do not need to change or influence my mood with food, drugs or alcohol. I am just happy to sit and be with my own thoughts and with myself and do not really need anything to make me feel better or good about myself.

If you had that mindset and really felt so comfortable within yourself, how difficult would it be too emotionally abuse you? It would be very difficult indeed. I can honestly say that the above passage is where I live with my thoughts now. I did not always hold these thoughts and it was only when I learnt and accepted certain things about myself and the world that I really started to take back control of it.

The Power of Meditation
For me it started with meditation, I know we hear so much about it don't we and we all wonder if we need to go to a guru or learn it from a book or an app. I learnt meditation from a self-help book. It was the shortest and best introduction to meditation I had ever read. I want to teach it to you now and it will only take a few seconds to learn.

Take yourself to a quiet or peaceful place where you will not be disturbed. Sit or lay down, now close your eyes and just be with your thoughts. Notice what thoughts come up and then practise clearing your mind. One of the best ways to do this is to slowly count backwards from 100 to 0 and just hear the words in your head and visualise them coming and going.

There, now if you do this you are meditating!!! That is it that is how you just start to practise calmness and start to take back control of all the erratic and rambling thoughts in your head. You only have to do it for a few minutes and the effects are quite incredible. To this day I will make sure that I meditate each day even if it is only for a few minutes. It is great for taking you away from all of the distractions of your life, social media, worries and concerns and you will come out of it feeling calmer and more focused. You can expand on your meditation pathway if you wish and there are lot of free videos online and apps and books that will teach you guided meditation.

This was to be a huge part of my self-healing and again it was another building block in getting back control of my own mind. For when I did this I realised that for the first time, I could just sit and be on my own and be calm and happy. I needed no one or nothing at that given time. It was a really empowering moment and for the first time, I felt that I was on to something good in my world. I was discovering mental and emotional self-efficiency. It was my first attempts into the world of meditation and relaxation that helped me to realise the fundamental importance of being able to focus and concentrate again. This was a skill that had eluded me and as I had my self-worth taken away, my ability to do those things that I used to hold of great value had also gone. Through using daily mediation, I started to read again and found that I had gained my ability to watch a whole documentary or film without the need to check my phone or social media every few minutes. Yes, it is incredible what people with Narcissistic intent can do to you. It was my desire to be able to just sit and be on my own and be happy with myself that had made me realise just how much of myself I had lost, even my ability to think for myself, make my own decisions and focus on a book for more than 5 minutes without being concerned that I was doing something wrong.

This period of healing can be quite difficult, as it does require you to seek total solitude and be equally comfortable with this as you are in the company of others.

Why do we need to be alone to self-heal?
You may be questioning why this step is such a major part of healing? Narcissists pray on your weak emotions, those parts of you that you reach out with, looking to connect to others with to feel good about who you are. When you need to feel loved, valued, happy, held, they will be there with arms outstretched hands and really make you feel whatever you need to feel. This is why their company and your connection will feel so good,

but you are yet to realise that it will come with a price. That price will be whatever they want it to be, money, your time, sex or whatever they need they will take, knowing that they are in a position to give you whatever emotional hit you need. For them it is a win-win contract, they can meet your needs by faking their true intention and then get what they want in return. They will remind you how great it is for you to have them in your life, time and time again and remind you what your life was like without them. But what if you could take away their greatest weapon? That weapon being "Your need to need something emotionally from others". If you did not possess this, they would be helpless and unable to feed off of you. So let us look at how we do this.

So what did you think you needed so badly?
So this is your time while you are self-healing to start to see what it was that you felt that you really needed and that this person gave you. Was it comfort, security, did they make you feel young and attractive again? Sit and write down all of the things that you felt that you needed that you felt they were providing. Now write next to each of these which emotions they hit, when you felt you were provided with each need. Was it happiness, security, comfort? Take a good look at all of these things you have written down and notice one thing about them. I guarantee you that they were all needs that produced emotions that you are capable of creating in your own mind. Even if they were material objects the reasons for needing those has an emotional bases. It is so important that you start to realise this now before you ever become tempted to fall into any of those emotional holes again. You see as humans we want certain things in life and those things which we desire always have an emotional basis. For example, we may feel that having a partner will bring us happiness, love and companionship. Or a new car will bring us respect, kudos, security. Every desire has an emotional need and the brain will often guide us towards those things that we see providing them, partially if those things say

and do the right thing to hit our emotional needs. Now when we start to analyse our needs and discover the emotional need behind them, we discover one incredible thing about them. None of our emotional needs can ever be bought off of a shelf, love, happiness comfort etc. They are products that you have created in your mind and the narcissist will see this and happily sell them to you. You need to start to become aware what your emotional needs are you need to start meeting them in a way which does not cost you in a negative or harmful way.

Learning to just sit and be, gave me the grounding to not want to be in any kind of relationship which would harm me. I become stronger and less reliant on others to provide or meet my emotional needs. It also made me go out and see those careers which were more in line with what I wanted to do. Now the emotions which were being met here for me were success, fulfilment, happiness and comfort. So once I had analysed what I wanted on an emotional level, I then started to work out how to get these things for myself and this was to be key to ensuring that I did not fall foul of a Narcissist again.

Now finding your emotional needs can be a very empowering exercise to take yourself through, however, you may have found that the exercise produced the opposite effect opposite. You may feel there could be areas of your life which you felt were too painful to deal with yourself so you let someone else deal with them for you. If this is true for you regarding your emotional needs then the next section is for you.

Dealing with Pleasure and pain
Pain like pleasure is a funny thing; we choose to attach pain to certain things if we feel we are going to not like them. But if you think about it, the pain is not actually real, we just imagine it is, then it feels real, so we allow our actions to be controlled by something powerful (our imagination) but not reality. Let me give you an example.

One of the things which I had always felt that I needed was help and support with at one point in my life was sorting out personal finances. It was not that I could not do it, it just used to bore me stupid so I attached pain to doing it and left as much of it as I could to other people. This was actually a weak area of mine and if I had not decided to take back control of this area of my life, it would have made me open to abuse. However, when it was just me alone in a room, I knew that now I had no choice but to sort them out myself and I did. It was boring and I discovered eloquent ways getting over this. One method was to find a trusted financial advisor and work with them. The other way was to break down the tasks and do them one by one. As I was on my own in this task, I just had to get on with it. This actually taught me even greater self-sufficiency and once again made me more secure as a person and less reliant on others. I had suddenly started to attach other thoughts to what represented pain to my world.

For many people being alone is a fear, even the word "alone" will strike fear into them and they will do anything to avoid it. But this is because they have associated too much pain to being alone already and now fear it. But actually when you stop and think about it, being alone won't kill you if you have to spend some time by yourself. I am not referring to long term isolation here, I mean having to be by yourself for a while. It is actually ok and yes while it might not be that great, you will not die of being in on a Friday night by yourself. However acknowledging that you can be by yourself and it will be ok is a logical thought, but unfortunately logic never defeats emotion.

Now what prevents people from taking certain causes of action are not the logical thoughts but our emotions. We can actually very easily affect our own emotions by the pictures and words we create in our own heads. When we create pictures and words in our head and give it some meaning, we call this a thought.

We then add meaning to the thoughts and it becomes a story which controls our emotions and we act, or fail to act because of it. For example, we think if we do not find a partner straight away we will be on our own for the rest of our lives. We then see future self as old and alone and feel pain. We then experience this story with meaning in our heads time and time again it affects our emotions before it ever happens and we then make a fear, which we perceive as pain. So we then have a painful fear of being alone. So then when the first person comes along who shows interest in you, you grab on to them whether they are good for you or not, just to make the pain go away and then fear losing them, as you believe that the pain will return. Then you become vulnerable to abuse due to your perceived pain levels of being alone again. When you create stories in your head you are doing nothing more than future pacing your own pain and making it worse than it ever could be. Another word for this is catastrophizing. Now can you see how just creating negative pictures and sounds in your head drives you to that place where you are vulnerable to abuse?

Now I was very fortunate and found self-healing in self-help and while this may not be for everyone I promise you that the foundation that you are looking to build on is the same for anyone who has ever been abused. You are looking for a real inner happiness and calmness and that only comes from a position of self-validation. A million people could all tell you a million times how amazing you are, but if you do not believe it, it is just noise and they are just words. You really need to start to find out who you are and what you enjoy. Some people I have met they told me that running or walking was their salvation and that getting out on their own every day meant that they felt good about who they were again. From personal experience, I found that eating right and exercise was a further great salvation. When I really got my concentration back, playing games such as chess and backgammon also helped me and I started to feel that great sense of achievement from accomplishing things I had missed in my world, cooking and working out, listening to the music I loved and reading. Now again I will defend all of these interests even though they are solitary activities and the reason for this is that they teach you how to think, focus and strategies and most importantly they do not require another person in your world at this time. Now do not get me wrong I am not saying that we never need anyone else ever again, we are not total solitary creatures and human connection is a great thing, but in self-healing from Narcissistic abuse we need to build up our inner resources and the only way we can do this, is to learn to sit and be and not need others. This is not self-isolation this is a period of self-healing where you are preparing yourself to be reborn. Remember your emotional needs are the greatest weapon the Narcissist will ever have. When we take our emotional needs out of the hands of the Narcissist, they are defenceless.

What is your story and what do you mean to yourself

I love films, books and drama series on TV. It is no accident that films and books and TV series have a vast amount of influence in the world and make billions and billions of pounds worldwide. Even piece of music is accompanied by great videos which tell stories. The truth of the matter is that we all love a story. From our childhood we were read stories, religious scripture contain great stories and even modern day urban myths are just great moral stories that guide us. From the time of the ancient Egyptians to today's manga and anime, we all love a story of some sort. So what has this got to do with self-healing I am sure you are thinking? Ok, several years ago I knew someone who very closely identified with the character Nancy from Oliver Twist. She adored the character from the film and I even witnessed her from time to time singing the song "As long as he needs me" which if you have ever listened to is a small tragedy within itself. Now this person was a victim of abuse and there was no doubt about it, she was also in love with the person who was abusing her. The problem was at that time, she had totally romanticised the relationship and the abuse. She saw herself as a tragic heroine in the same vein as Nancy from the story Oliver and we all know what happened to her. No matter how bad the abuse got, still the words of the song played in her head "As long as he needs me". This was her story and in as much, she was playing the part of a tragic character who was heading for disaster. Then something changed, I was never sure what it was and never did find out. All that I knew was that one day she just changed the story of her life and the song in her head and left her abuser. She almost seemed to transform overnight, she dressed differently and looked and spoke differently, and it was as if she had just started writing a new script and story for herself. Now earlier on I spoke about the Narcissist being the writer, director and lead actor of their own and your world, in order to control the action and you. Now when I met up again with this person it was as if she had just decided to fire the director, writer and producer and the entire cast and started starring in their own brand new TV series. This new series had a new set, new characters, costume designer and the scriptwriter had brought humour and adventure into this series. It was amazing their old abuser could not even get a bit part anymore and their ratings soon slipped and their show was cancelled. Now go on be honest, who enjoyed that story? It was a good one wasn't it, it was a great story of change, it put images in your head and it had an upbeat ending that I bet made you smile. The best thing was about that story was that it was completely true. Now let me ask you a question, what is your story and are you the one writing the script these days? This is a very powerful question to sit and think about and not one that you may have ever asked yourself before. We tend not to think of our life or world as a story, but if we did would you be happy to sit and watch it or read it? Maybe you would and if that is the case, what does that say about you if you feel that your life is a tragedy and a drama that makes you cry. We are often attracted to certain things in the world or literature and film, I love to read books or watch films with intelligent heroes who have great minds, Jack Ryan and Robert Langdon are two names that just spring to mind and that tells you something about me and how I like to problem solve. I mention this as sometimes we are drawn to create a story in an image we desire. The person I mentioned was obviously drawn the Character of Nancy from Oliver and maybe when she had a chance of becoming that person. I am not saying this is the case, but that person would talk about other tragic characters from literature and history and felt a connection with them. So I will ask you the same question, what is the story of your life, are you someone who sees themselves as a victim or unlucky in love and life? We are all capable of writing our own story and this is actually something that we do, but don't acknowledge it. I have sat with a number of people who will tell me their stories like this, "Well that is just how my life runs bad luck every day," or "If it is going to happen it will happen to me". I always think to myself when I hear this, "You are just writing a rubbish script for yourself every day and then playing that role and then surprised when things go wrong". In my life I have to admit I have met more than my fair share of Narcissists, I do not think that this is awful or bad or my terrible luck. I just acknowledge that in my life story I have been aware enough to spot these people and been able to study them up close, so I can now help others to avoid them and make sure they are not abused by them. You could say that I am using these experiences to write a better story for myself and those around me. If you really had all of the resources of a top TV or film producer, what story would you write for yourself? Would it be an intelligent comedy, a fun packed adventure a tale of triumph over adversity? Or would you just write yet another sad tale of abuse, misery and sadness? Stop and think about this for a minute because at this time of writing I know that you possess the most incredible resource, more powerful than any Hollywood movie. You possess your mind and your imagination and with this incredible tool, you are able to start rewriting your script and your story right away. It does not matter who you are, how old you are, what has happened to you before this time, you can pick up that virtual pen or laptop in your head and start to pen an award-winning blockbuster right now. Your life is yours to own and as soon as you realise that it is time to fire all the cast and crew that have been working against you, you can start a great new chapter, a new film or brilliant new TV series starring you. It can be whatever you want it to be and you can bring the right kind of people into it to share it with you and write out those you no longer want to see on set. Your life story should only be penned by you and you alone when you are self-healing. I knew at the lowest point in my world that one day something brilliant would come out of my worst experiences; I was not sure what, a new type of therapy, a book maybe! Write your script from today and make it a good one, when you do this, you do the most powerful thing of all; you stop other people writing your script for you.

Attaching meaning to your story

One of the greatest films I have ever seen is a film called "Scent of a woman" with Al Pacino. In the film Al Pacino plays a grumpy, blind ex-Lieutenant Colonel Frank Slade, who has to spend the Thanksgiving weekend with a local college boy, Charlie played by Chris O'Donnell. Charlie, who has problems of his own, has agreed to look after Frank, while Frank's family get some well-needed respite from him. The weekend does not go as Charlie thought it would and Frank has plans that lead them both to New York. Now I do not want to give away any of the plot of this film and if you have never seen it, I would recommend it. Why do I mention it, well it is one of my favourite films and the story has great meaning. There are two stories running at once, Charlies and Franks, they intertwine and both central characters play a part in helping each other. The story has great meaning such as friendship, support, overcoming adversity, standing up to bullies, never giving up, accepting change, there are no such things as limitations. The film is rich in meaning but to be honest, these are the meanings that I have chosen to attach to this film. Someone else may see the film and hate it, or they may decide that there are other meanings to the movie, political, social or financial. I do not see any of these; I see the meanings that I want to attach to it.

This is what we do with films and this is what we do with our lives, we attach meaning to it. Now, by and large, this is ok, but it is when we decide to attach the wrong kind of meaning to our story that we run into problems. So how do we know what meaning we have attached to our life so far? Well first we need to look at what has gone on in our lives so far and acknowledge this in the following manner

Acceptance and changing your story
There are things that we have to accept in our world. We have to accept and acknowledge who we have been up until now and how we have behaved due to our experiences and thoughts. Your emotions and subsequent actions have dictated your life and you have done this by attaching meaning to your story.

You have to accept your past story may have been one of dependence and need. You may have needed to feel wanted, loved or protected for all of the wrong reasons. You may have been tied into a romantic notion or been listening and believing what other people have told you without question. Now it is so important within the healing process that we start to look to those things which we may have done in order to start moving forwards and see ourselves for who we are. One of the best ways of doing this is to acknowledge that you were not born with any of your emotional needs. I know it is an incredible step forward to take a huge step back and acknowledge that you were not born with any. You had physical needs, food and water but everything else in life you were taught, including your emotional needs. Now everyone was raised differently and we all process our upbringing in a way which either empowers us or gives us a need. My parents were both busy people and gave a lot of their time to work and partly due to his lifestyle I lost my

Father at a young age. I decided that as sad as it was to never fully know my Father I would not let it be an issue for me in my own life. It was a choice that I had in how I wanted to process a traumatic part of my own childhood. As I grew older I knew that I could let it be part of my negative story (I am the man who never knew his dad) and attach meaning to that (I never had a strong male role model, so I can excuse myself for any behaviour I wish). However, I made a conscious decision that it would not be part of my life story. It was definitely part of the reality of my life, but it would not become part of my story or psychological makeup and if it was it would be a part that empowered me. I attached some great meaning to this part of my life and that meaning was (I learnt independence from a young age and how to stand on my own two feet).

We all face choices every day and it is when we realise this that we can start to grasp the concept that we can indeed alter our story, even if it is our past that we are looking at. You cannot change your past, but you can change the way that you feel about it. It is a choice for you to make today, right now. Your past up until now has just become your past story and you need to start viewing it through a new lens. If you wish you can see your past and your actions as really important lessons that have taken you to this point in your life right now. You do not have to reject your past, but accept that it exists and that it does not have to be your future. We can often make this mistake and feel that our future will be the same as the past, so in order to accept that you can heal and move on you need to accept that your life will be different from this point right now. When we stop doing this and keep our thoughts focused in the present we are much more capable of dealing with our lives and what is about to unfold next. You may in the past have always reached out to others for reassurance and to have your emotional needs met and this may have caused you to be vulnerable to the Narcissistic treatment of other people. If this is the case then it is time to start accepting that was your old story. It is time that you changed your story.

You have to stop and think, what does my story mean to me and what am I going to do about it!

Self-healing technique

This is another therapeutic technique that has taught many people who need to selfheal. This technique is very effective and works very quickly as within it you have to acknowledge those real reasons why you have been abused, take complete ownership of this reason and then take action to ensure that we never let it happen again.

First I want you to be really honest here with yourself. Not let yourself off the hook but be honest about why you have been a victim of abuse. Remember people only treat you how you let them. If you are to ever move on you have to go through this technique and start to fully selfheal.

Step 1: Admit that there is something about you that needs to be different in order to never be abused again. What is it called? Is it your fear of challenging others, fear of displeasing people? Are you afraid of being on your own? Take some time and consider the reasons that you allow the abuse to continue for and write them down. Name them for what they are, Vanity, fear of rejection, scared of being alone. Whenever comes to mind write it down.

Step 2: Now you have called it out, I want you to observe it in action. Think about how it controls your life and your world. Think of those times that others have been able to control and manipulate you because of this reason. Did you just let others take things from you, as you were scared they would leave you? Were you abused at work, as you believe that you are not strong enough to stand up and defend yourself? It is important that at this stage we stop blaming anyone and everyone for this and just acknowledge that this is our problem and ours alone to deal with.

Step 3: Now I want you to make a change to your world and mind and admit that something must be done to change this. Visualise what will happen if you do not. How bad will your life be in 5 years if you do not change this? What will still be happening to you if you do not change things starting from this moment?

Step 4: Now that you have admitted that you have this problem and can see the harm that it is causing to you and unless you change it things will only get worse you have to deal with it. It has presented itself before you and is yours to take charge of and deal with. So now I am going to ask you the 7 most important and empowering questions you have ever been asked to deal with this.

Healing from your main issue or self-concern

Ask yourself these questions and write down the answers

1. What are you going to do about it?
2. When are you going to do it?
3. How are you going to do it?
4. If you don't what will happen
5. If you do what will happen and what will stop?
6. Who will support you?
7. What is the first thing that you are going to do today to change it?

Step 5: These questions are a great guide to moving you forward in your world and this is the one time I am going to say that you need to stop reading this book and go and make just one step to completing the first action that you identified in this list. You may have said find a new job, seek help from friends, find professional support, or even just join a club. Whatever it was, I want you to go and do it now. For this is the only way that we ever truly self-heal, we do it by taking positive affirmative action regarding those things in our life which need healing.

Why you have to take action and plan your own future

We have to take action and this is so important regarding healing as when we take those first few steps we start to create a positive emotional new pathway in our life. We start to see that there is a future where we can function and exist in a completely new way, free of the pressures which we may have previously felt. We start to see that we can feel whole or function fully again. It is so important that you start to create a positive new pathway for yourself.

If we don't have a plan and see a future that will bring us happiness then we are less likely to take any actions towards our new goals. But when we do, we will find the whole healing process so much easier and quicker as we know where we are going.

When dealing with Narcissistic abuse and healing from it, we may not have been aware of just how controlling someone was in our lives and the only future that we may have felt we had was one which they created for us. If we have allowed this to happen then all that we are doing is fulfilling someone else's goals and dreams and end up not having a strong enough vision for our own future.

Why you can feel hopelessly lost without the Narcissist in your life

The very fact that Narcissists will have been leading and guiding and controlling you can actually make it so hard for some people to break away from abusers. This is because their abuser has been the one dictating the path and some people fear without this person that they have no future or do not know where they are going. If this is something that you are experiencing then be very aware of where you are at the moment, as you could not be more wrong. Narcissists love to control your future and will often tell you what is going to happen and when and for what reasons. This is a great way of securing your compliance and why you may feel that deep sense of loss and indeed lack of direction without them, as they always seemed to have the map and knew what was happening.

It is almost like the captain of a ship telling everyone that they had a map to a great paradise island and if everyone just listened to them, did as they said, it would all turn out great and you would all reach paradise together. Of course, this destination is never reached and you have to just keep on following their orders and be aware that the compass may point North one day and then South the next and then back to North the next, but by now you have just become used to following their orders. After a while, this gives them carte blanche to pretty much do as they like, with you accepting whatever they do or say, because they have reassured you that they are the best person to lead and know where they are going. Narcissists will do anything to keep control of the future and assure you are browbeaten into giving up all control of your future. It is a fact that many people will just feel more comfortable to be led in this life and also be quite fearful of making decisions in case they get it wrong. But what we know now regarding Narcissists is that they do not possess these fears so will just go ahead and blindly drag you where they like, while they still continue to tell you it is all happening for the right reasons.

But if you stop and scratch the surface here, you will see that actually, it is nothing more than a ruse to just manipulate you further into bending to their will. There really is no map and anyone can create whatever future they desire for themselves. Narcissists are just great at saying things with such force and conviction (Great storytellers remember) and then attaching meaning to it. For a very long time, I was led to believe that my future direction of my life was going to be living in a foreign country away from my family and friends. I was sold the story time and time again and the story was given meaning by the person selling it to me, through alarming me that their health was a factor attached to this story. It was a very clever way of having me commit to a future that I did not really want; as if this was something which I did not agree to then I was actually going to be causing them physical pain. So after a while, I was sold the story and even made images of it in my head and could fully visualise someone else`s dream. I did not want it, but there it was spread out before me and the alternative was a person in pain if I did not commit to it.

Then one day I found myself alone and my whole future had felt like it had been taken away from me. Now as relieved as I was to be away from someone who had caused me so much pain, to my amazement I really wanted them back!! Now one of the main reasons for this was that I could not see a future without them. This other future had been imprinted on my mind and I knew that it would never happen without them. Amazingly enough, I had been taken in by the old classic sales technique, the take-away. The "take away" is one of the strongest techniques that can stop people from healing from abuse from Narcissists. Narcissists know this because they know that when you go back to them, it will temporarily make the emotional pain stop. The take away works like this. You are briefly given something lovely in your life to hang on to, you may not have even wanted it to begin with, but after a while, you get used to it and then when you get used to it you start to value it. Then without warning, it is gone and you will feel like you are totally alone and lost without whatever it was. A car salesman tried this one me one day. He let me drive a new car he was selling; I drove it, loved it and really wanted it. He then drove mine and came back handed me my keys and said, no deal there are too many things wrong with your car. I was really upset, I had sold myself on this bright shiny new car and now I had lost it. Let us be honest I never really had it, but in my mind, I thought I did and that was all that mattered. Also, I had thought I had found my dream car straight away and did not have to spend the day car hunting.

I had attached so many positives to this new car which made it even more desirable. The salesman then said, well maybe I could give you something for your old car. I had a moment of clarity and realisation and told him I would think about it. I went to another more established garage where they test drove my car, had professional engineers look at it. They told me there was nothing wrong with my car and offered me twice what the first salesman had. Obviously, I took their offer.

When you are used to having your future mapped out or another future repeatedly sold to you by those who only wish to manipulate you, they are aware just how painful it can be for you to have it taken away. Just remember, it was not your future, it was only a story they had attached meaning, to make you want it. Like my car, there was nothing wrong with anything in it internally or externally, but I was told there were loads of things wrong with it and it was worthless. Actually, it was a great car and in great condition and had miles of life left in it.

We can so often fall victim to the false stories that Narcissists feed us time and time again and miss the negative meanings which they are attaching to them and us. Remember keeping us down and making us believe there is something wrong with us is a huge weapon in the Narcissist arsenal. At the same time they are exploiting us and making our unconscious wounds visible, they are selling us the other false story of how lucky we are to have them in our lives. It is only when we stop believing them that we wake up to their manipulations and start to live as we were meant to be.

 The most painful period in my life came when I allowed a Narcissist to convince me that there were so many things wrong with me and that I was falling apart. Their manipulations were constant and daily and nothing I did could make it right and I was told no matter what action I took, "it just made it worse". Of course, when I went to a real professional who was able to give me a real diagnose, they made me realise that actually I was just fine and there was nothing wrong with me at all. I had just been made to repeatedly feel bad and worthless every single day, as it allowed a Narcissist to control and manipulate me and take control of my future. It also allowed them to behave however they liked and forgive themselves for their actions, claiming I had caused it. This was the classic Narcissistic trick of cutting me and crying out in pain, again and again, and again. It was only when I took the reins and ejected them from my life that I realised none of this was true and I could start to self-heal and plan my own great future. I had not realised it, but I myself had been a victim of Narcissistic abuse.

Your future has not yet happened yet and it is down to you to decide just what and who is going to be in it. So now start heading towards your bright future and make it a fantastic one.

4. MENTAL MARTIAL ARTS, HOW TO BE MENTALLY STRONG AND FIGHT

Within this next section, I want you to look on me as a martial arts instructor for the mind. I want to train you to become a Jedi in self-awareness, get your black belt in mental self-defence and become a Ninja in Mental self-defence. I am going to teach you how to become more focused and centred on who you are so that you can stand and fight and defeat the worst kinds of Narcissist. It is time that you learnt to defend yourself and fight back. When dealing with a Narcissist, you have to be prepared for combat and fighting with the mind in every way is the same as a real battle, you have to be ready to avoid and block strikes, you also need to have counter moves, such as sweeps and throws and you also need to be prepared to strike back. Always remember as Sun Zu said in the art of war, "All warfare is based on deception" and "every battle is won before it is even fought" The difference between you and the Narcissist is that they are always in a state of readiness for battle and will devote time and effort to winning. For the Narcissist the psychological battlefield is a fertile ground for them. It is one they have spent years of their lives living, winning and thriving in. It is a territory that you need to become familiar with if you ever hope to compete and win.

The first step of winning any kind of psychological manipulation is to understand that territory, your own mind. The greater your grip on who you are and your sense of self then the greater the chance that you have of winning this psychological battle

How I learnt to fight

On, reflection I am aware that I have been a victim of Narcissistic abuse many times throughout my life. On some occasions, I spotted the attack coming, blocked it and verbally swept the legs from under my attacker straight away. Other times I was slow to respond to an attack as I was distracted by them and sucker punched. However, the worst kind of attack was the one that I saw coming and choose to ignore it. This kind of abuse was totally my fault as I did not want to believe that this particular person would do this to me. I allowed them to infiltrate my thoughts, cloud my beliefs on their actions and my sense of self and then let them repeatedly punch and kick me to the ground and then carry on their assault. There was only one person to blame for this, not the Narcissist, not society, not social media or my parents. No the only person at fault here was me!! I know that my real turning point came when I experienced first-hand just what the costs could be of allowing myself to be deceived. For me, the costs were almost, my sense of self-worth, my finances, career progression and nearly even my sanity.

We are all acutely aware of the effects of emotional abuse and need to consider and discuss some of the other far wider reaching effects of it. For example, how can abuse affect your drive and ambition and ability to perform at a high level? Narcissist abuse will leave a trail of confusion in your mind that can be created through someone distorting your reality on a daily bases. With my own personal experiences, I am only too aware of what the costs "could" have been. As even though my journey has been painful and produced losses, I was able to heal (quickly) and recover my identity. I also learnt not only how to survive, but also how to thrive amongst Narcissistic people and beat them at their own game.

Lesson 1: Wake up from Naivety

1. Open your eyes

This is the most important step of all and it is more of a mindset and a philosophy, rather than a tactic or strategy. You have to accept that we are going through the looking glass here and you will need to do this if you want to become mentally tough and be able to defend yourself. You need to become acutely aware that your current way of thinking is, all wrong!! Yes, you need to stop believing that everyone you meet is decent, nice and is there to support you and help you and will always have your best intentions at heart. If you reject or cannot take on board this new philosophy, or find it is too difficult or hard to process, then you will not make the changes that you need to. You will also spend the rest of your life a victim and abused by Narcissists and continue to make excuse after excuse as each blow falls upon you, either psychologically, emotionally, financially or even physically. If you only ever learn one thing from me then please learn this one lesson. Naivety is the greatest weapon that the Narcissist will use against you. No matter what they say, do, promise or convince, there only intent will be to manipulate you into doing whatever they want. That is it, end of story, if you look for something else from them (they were abused, confused, had a bad start in life), know that while you are looking for an excuse for them, they will most likely be going through your bank account and emptying it at the same time. From my own experience every time I have ever lowered my defences either at work, socially, or in any new relationships; there has always been a Narcissist within the vicinity just waiting to get beyond my defences and start their evil work.

The problem is that opening our eyes and accepting that monsters really are living amongst us is a really hard thought to take on board. We don't want to believe it and very little supports these thoughts. Society and the better angels of the world have us believe that everyone is essentially good. Some of the most recognised and oldest writings of the world teach us the ways of forgiveness and embracing those who would do us harm. But this is not always the case as there are those who recognise society's rules that we are taught and believe that we are easy prey as we follow them. For those of you who follow societies rule to the letter and adopt this passive approach towards abuse, it just allows Narcissists to continue to abuse you and then beg your forgiveness, then abuse you further. The saying is so true that asking for forgiveness is so much easier than asking for permission. You have to recognise that there is an invisible war going on around you every day and you do need to open your eyes to it and learn to defend yourself and how to fight.

My approach to any dispute was always to talk and resolve. As a professional mediator and negotiator, I realise that our greatest assets are our ability to listen, see things from another's perspective and then talk and find a route that helps both sides. Within the mediation the real gift being our chance to improve our relationship with another person, so that a dispute will not arise again and if it does we now have a solid foundation to build upon. Over the years I have perfected my negotiation skills and there are elements of them that have served me well when dealing with Narcissistic people. However, we have to remember that we are not dealing with a normal group of people here. We are dealing with those who will lie, steal, cheat, abuse and break any boundary or rule in order to get their way. So the conventional rules are not always going to work. You need to take your game to the next level and it starts with this important step of recognising that monsters are real and do live among us.

2. Why is this first step the hardest?
How do we allow these people to swim within our pool, unrecognised or challenged? Simple we don't want to see them. What follows is an example of why we struggle to accept there are those in the world who we cannot deal with conventionally.

They were the sweetest nicest person you ever could have wished to meet. They were loved by their friends, family and the local community and always did good work that helped others around them. Their language was clean, they hardly drank, did not smoke and presented very nicely. They had a positive and liberal attitude of acceptance of tolerance to all. They had high standards and never openly spoke ill of others. Everyone was considered within their company and was taken care of. No one ever held any bad thoughts or feelings towards them and they breezed through life with a smile upon their face.

How difficult would it be to recognise and then accept that this person was the cruellest and most manipulative Narcissist you had ever met? So let us look at the same person when the doors were closed and they took off their perfectly painted on mask.

They secretly had vile nicknames for those around them and constantly put others down when they were out of earshot. They betrayed deep confidences and used personal informa-tion they gained to manipulate those within their circle. They would actively and willingly destroy lives and others relation-ships and cry out in pain as they did, saying it was the fault of others. Their lies knew no boundaries and they were relentless within their psychological torture of those who they saw as having served their purpose. They would use any tactic to get what they wanted and knew that the more harmful and cutting their words became the more effective they were. They saw and used people as nothing more than stepping stones to achieving their social and financial goals. They could smell others fears and anxieties like a shark could smell blood and when they did they would move in for the kill and exploit vulnerable relation-ships, low self-worth and promise to be the cure for all their ills and woes. However when a bigger prize caught their eye, then it was time to start their game again. They only had one fear, being exposed and being found out; but believed that others around them were too stupid to ever suspect them. However, they knew that they were safe as no one ever saw them without their mask on.

That person is not a fictional character. This person exists and could live next door to you. They could be your manager, work colleague or friend. You may even be living with them or have grown up with them as a member of your family. Always remember the words of the French author Charles Baudelaire "The greatest trick the Devil pulled was convincing the world that he did not exist"

Lesson 2: The Power of reality

1. You don't know anything or anyone and you never really will
To say that this pathway I have taken in life has turned me into a realist is an understatement. I have recently been accused of being a realist in the extreme and it's a label I wear with pride. Reality is the greatest weapon of all when it comes to defending yourself against abuse. As you will see the strong use of reality and staying within it can form the bases of your defence strategy.

2. How to become grounded in reality: Building a strong defensive fighting position with it
You need to hold only one thought with an identified Narcissist. "I hold no trust around anything you say or do". That needs to be your new mantra. This needs to be the new defensive stance that you take whenever you have any interaction with them. They will try every trick in the book, gifts, guilt sympathy, over-familiarity and friendliness. They may even offer to help and lighten the load by taking things off of your hands. All of these tactics are meant to win you over so they can distort your view of who they really are and their aims. You need to keep a clear sharp eye on who they are and what their aim and intentions really are. So to master less one, breaking from naivety you need to have a solid mantra or line that you can repeat that

will always remind you of where you need to keep your mind-set. The line that I use to use was, "You were unfaithful and lied about it and that is all I need to know about you"

3. Start to build your strong emotional fighting muscle

It is here where you are going start learning to fight and you're first, biggest and toughest opponent is going to be yourself. You need to change and you need to accept and acknowledge that what you do is all wrong. If you are reading this then you need to change. I am not just talking about changing what you say and do; I am talking about changing who you are. This is the tough-est part and listening to your friends, family, work colleagues who say "No" you are great as you are, you're a lovely person is the worst thing you could ever listen to. I was once told, by someone who themselves had strong Narcissist tendencies, that I was "too nice" and on reflection, they were totally cor-rect. I was far too "nice". I was always thankful of that comment and needed to hear it. It is worth noting that they told me this as an attempt to get me to take a strong line with others, which would then work against me, so they themselves could appear in a better light. That was the real Narcissist boss at work there, empower someone to take a hard line against others and when it backfires, seek the glory by taking the softer approach and appear as a great defender. However their comment still held water, these days I would reframe it as I was still "too naïve and trusting" to see the trap they were laying. Always be wary of those who seek to keep you as you are, or attempt to shape and mould you into something else. This is not where you need to take yourself when I talk of change. By changing who you are I am looking at you becoming more aware and focused, having greater emotional control. Finding your centre and achieving that greater sense of self whilst being in touch with reality. You won't get that by being nicer, harder, softer and considerate or any of the other things that people will tell you. You also won't achieve it by staying the same as you are. Be assured what I am going to teach you, will change who you are to the core and that is good, as you need to change.

The first step here is to take control of your own mind in any situation. You can now see and accept that you are constantly under attack from others 24/7 with their distortions and deletions and attempting to fog your mind with their lies. Now in order to do this, we need to start practising moving ourselves from a state of emotion to a state of logic on more frequent bases. It is one thing to be passionate about those things in life we enjoy, but a whole other thing to not let ourselves become carried away with our emotions and get caught up in others promises and speeches. You need to become someone who looks at the actions taken and the results generated, rather than the words which are spoken. It must be true for you that actions, indeed speaks clearer and louder than words. You need to move your mindset from foolishly trusting to inquisitive and investigatory. This may be a new route for you to take and you will find it strangely empowering and enlightening when you start to first start to undertake it. One of the first things that you will also notice will be those who immediately attempt to pervert you from this course of action. Those who will say, "don`t you trust me?" or "why so many questions?" Anyone who is in your life and is a decent person will be ok with your questioning them, it is those who shy away from giving answers or attempt to fog or distort that you need to be aware of. As a mediator and crisis negotiator, when working for the police I am often put into the role of investigator, asking questions and digging deeper to get to the heart of a person's reason for their actions. Who, where, when, what and how are the best tools that I have at my disposal and I keep them sharp and use them daily. When you respond in this way to people, you are putting yourself in the driving seat and directing the conversation as you need to. This one act alone allows you to get out of that emotional state and bring yourself to a position of logic. It is only when we start to do this that we can see others for who they are.

4. Using reality as a defensive weapon

It is one thing to accept reality and acknowledge it and a whole other thing to use it. When you can fully comprehend and take on board the philosophy of lesson one, then lesson two is much easier to comprehend. As Robert Green states in The 50th Power, you need to convert to realism. Reality is a state that many of us avoid as it is way too painful. If you are in or have ever been in any kind of relationship with a Narcissist, they will have attempted to bend and shape your reality to serve themselves. One of their greatest weapons against you is making you believe things about yourself or other people that are not true, either through Gas lighting or changing the narrative. Now they can be very convincing as both of these when used to too such as degree will start to make you question everything about yourself. If you are someone who is rooted in reality then you are going to be much harder to manipulate. It is all about having that complete emotional control and staying out of the drama. Your lesson here is to keep your eyes open to the world in all of your encounters and to be aware of those who would manipulate you and try and stop you from achieving this. Be aware of those who preach positivity, honesty and trust and use words like negativity, paranoia and become defensive over questioning. You are not being negative, or paranoid you are just starting to open your eyes and they will try and close them again.

5. Base your decisions on a person's actions and deeds, never their words

One of the most important elements of this step is to only judge someone on what you absolutely know to be true and nothing else. Narcissistic people are very creative and can weave and tell amazing tales of past glories and what they will do for you. It is so easy to be taken in by their stories as they will tell us what we wish to hear every time. Remember they have been watching and listening and will know just what you want. So we need to put our trust on hold here and actually, wait to see what consistent long term behaviour someone displays before we open our door and let them in. I have often told people, to wait until I produce a set of results for them before they believe me. It is very easy to act strong and confident and Narcissists exude that natural charm and rely on it to carry them through. Real and genuine people do not need to do this and will let their actions do the talking.

Again this is so important for you to do this, as it starts to shape and focus your own belief system. When you convert to realism within your mind, it will make you more grounded and stable and you will start to look for and wait for the solid outcomes of people`s actions rather than their words. Here is a simple technique you can do right now that will strengthen your mind and help you see others for who they are. First, think of someone who you think maybe manipulating you and now remove from your thoughts about them anything they have ever told you about their past. Now also remove anything they have said that you have not witnessed first-hand or had solid evidence of. Now remove anything from your mind that they have promised you, but are yet to deliver. Now just view them based solely on their actions and behaviours. What does this tell you about them? Do you really not know them at all? Is their greatness based entirely on their words and tales? Have they ever displayed within their actions any of the things that they have told you they pride themselves on? Now go ahead and list all the deeds, actions and behaviours they have displayed in front of you. This is the reality of the person who you know. This is who they really are and this is how they will always be. If you're looking at a piece of paper that displays someone, who you just do not recognise, or at least recognise from their words it is time to re-think this relationship through and re-evaluate it.

6. Moving Narcissists from distortion to reality (Leg Sweep)

This is such a strong counter move to use against a Narcissist as it will sweep the legs away from their attack on you. You have to start to question anything that you think sound suspicious and you need to do it quickly and in the company of the Narcissist. As when you do this technique it will also work as a great counter-attack, so you can quickly confront them with solid evidence. It is a technique that I have effectively used many times in the past and always works. I will give you an example. Many years ago I used to spend time with someone who had strong manipulative tendencies and was always whispering in my ear various stories that he had overheard or been part of. One day he came to see me at work and casually dropped into the conversation that another friend of mine had been running me down all night. In a moment of reality seeking, I grabbed the phone and telling them I was going to phone my friend and ask why he had been running me down started to dial his number. The person who had told me this immediately panicked and started backing down and started saying all sorts of things like, well he may have been talking about someone else, or he may have meant it as a joke. He was faced with reality and it swept the legs from under him. This is one of the biggest fears that a Narcissist ever face, as you are totally destabilizing their argument and this allows you to see how thin it really is. Always remember most manipulative arguments when viewed are like paper walls. From one side they look solid, tall and strong, but if you view them from another angle they are paper thin and you can easily tear them down. To do this, you need to always challenge what you have been told straight away and go into action to seek the evidence for yourself. You have to be the truth seeker and find the reality within what you have been told.

Lesson 3: Strong mindset, strong body

1. How to develop a stronger mindset

So how do we develop a stronger mind and more to the point how do we know when we have developed one? One of the best ways that you can develop a strong mind is actually through the way that you use your physical body. Now, this may sound to you as though the reverse should be true. As we see that strong-willed and assertive people possess strong body language. However, what I am about to teach you are some very powerful short cuts that you can use to strengthen your mind and if you practise it enough will become second nature to you. I have used these techniques many times when dealing with difficult situations and people. I have also taught them to other people on crisis management and negotiation training courses. You see there is a strong correlation between where and how you physically position yourself and how you actually feel. We know that when we stand with our head lowered our eyes down and our back arched that we feel weak, disempowered and maybe even a little bit sad. Try it now and hold the pose for a while and see how it affects your emotions. This may even take you back to when you were a child and you were being told off, you see the mind will associate a certain physical position with a memory and you will then start to emotionally feed into the poor memory.

2. Taking a positive stand

Now it is time in your life that you took a stand and started to produce a different set of results for yourself and one of the best ways of doing this is by ensuring that you are fully in control of your feelings. Remember on some levels when you're dealing with Narcissists, you are preparing for war and before you go into battle, you need to have the correct mindset and indeed body posture. So now I want you to try a new experience, one that will make you feel different about yourself and your capabilities. First stand up straight, so straight that you are almost arching your back. You will be surprised when you check your posture in a mirror that actually you are not standing up straight even when you think you are. Now pull your shoulders back and hold this pose. How long is it since you decided to walk through life like this? Now walk around, it may actually feel like an effort at first and to be honest it will be. Standing up for yourself does take effort, both physical and mental. Now roll your eyes to the top of your head and smile. Now hold this pose for a few seconds and notice how this makes you feel. Are you feeling stronger and more capable, do you feel able to calmly talk to someone who has been standing in the way of your dreams?

Now I want you to go back to your old usual, beaten down position. Notice how that feels for a minute, you probably do not feel good and are accessing old negative memories. Ok now snap out of that and go back into your new confident pose. Back straight, shoulders back and roll your eyes to the top of your head and smile. Again notice what thoughts you are accessing about yourself and how much better you feel about your ability to have a greater level of control over your world?

3. Stepping forward

A large part of our world is often shaped by other people and the stories that they tell. It can also be shaped positively or negatively by those role models that we choose. Recently a client had been feeling very low and told me how whenever they see or hear a tragic story they put themselves into the thoughts of the person who they are reading about. In this particular instance, they had been reading about someone whose child was critically ill. Every time they thought of this story they put themselves into the role of the parent, what would they be feeling at this time and how would it affect them. Essentially they were living this person's life and taking on all of their problems and worries as well as her own. As you can imagine this was one of the major areas of concern for her and the reason was she was low in mood. Now when we encounter Narcissistic and abusive people, they will use every opportunity to lower our mood and put us into the role and mindset of someone with low self-esteem, who cannot stand up for themselves or fight back. Have you ever encountered someone who is usually quite strong, yet when they come into contact with a certain person they appear to almost change into another person altogether. That is because that person has conditioned them to be this way. They have repeatedly made them feel bad about themselves and every time that they encounter that person, their mood is lowered and they just feel bad in their company. Most narcissists will know that this is the route to absolute power, making the other person feel bad, just for being them. So this is where you draw the line and again start to change the game on them. Up until now, you may have never have felt that you possessed the confidence to step away from abuse and certainly not have ever felt that you possessed a strong enough mindset to change the direction of your life. But you don't have to, because you probably know someone who does and can. This is where we are going to let other people's brilliant strengths and strategies work for us. What I am about to teach you is quite possibly one of the most powerful mind strengthening techniques ever. You need to be really careful when using this technique so choose your role models very carefully as it will have a profound effect upon your thinking. So before you start this technique I want you to think of someone who you believe has the emotional and physical strength to overcome those obstacles in life that you are currently facing. Maybe this is someone who you know possess great self-respect and thinks well of themselves. This person who you are thinking of is capable of remaining calm and standing up for themselves and will not allow others to manipulate or control them. This may be a person that you know well or it may even be a fictional character, it can work just as well either way. Just make sure that the person you are choosing is a good person and decent. Make it someone who exudes those good qualities that you also wish to hold. Ok when you have thought of that person I want you to work through this technique

Stand up, (probably best to make sure you are doing this at home or at least in a private place) and imagine that this person is standing in front of you. Really use your incredible imagination and just imagine that they are actually in the room with you.

Now take a step closer to them and ask them for their help. They are going to smile, nod and say yes as they value you.

Now in a moment, I am going to ask you to take a step forward into them, so you can learn exactly what it is like to live in their mind. But before you do, just think about this person. Consider how they think, what are their thoughts like, may be totally different to yours?

Ask yourself these questions. How do they feel about themselves? How do they feel about other people who they know? How do they listen to others and how do they respond? There are no wrong answers here, you are making these decisions on what you have seen them do.

Now when you feel ready imagine that you can take a step forward so that you are inside of them. You are able to step into their body and know exactly what it is like to be them. You will know how they feel, how they think and would respond to people. Now you have done this, you really know how it feels to think like and be them.

Ask yourself some questions about your current situation and see what answers start to come up. Notice what different answers they come up with and also notice how those new empowered answers make you feel.

What are you able to accomplish now and what are you able to do differently in your life that you have never been able to do, until now?

This technique is so powerful that if you use it on a regular basis, then you will start to create positive new neural pathways in your brain that will give you the ability to start thinking differently. But always remember choose your role models carefully and wisely.

Lesson 4: Psychological warfare

Ok, now we are going to start to move over to a very dark area of mental martial arts, psychological warfare. This is the area where the Narcissists mind lives and breathes. It is their playground, their home territory and you need to learn the landscape, not only as well as them, but better than them.

1. Gaslighting

There has been so much already written about this very abuse and harmful tactic already, so I will break it down into very simple terms. Gaslighting is the process of altering a person's reality in order to make them doubt themselves and their own sanity. It is a highly manipulative act and the term comes from a 1944 movie called Gaslight, within the film a husband causes his wife to question herself and her reality. It is such a powerful tool in the psychological arsenal of the Narcissist that I could have given the subject its own chapter. Gaslighting will often start with someone being told that there is something wrong with them; there is a constant verbal negative reinforcement which plants the seeds of doubt within someone`s mind. For example, if someone tells you "You keep forgetting things don't you?" When I joined a new organisation, I was told by a Narcissistic manger that the old department that I used to run for my previous company "Had a very bad name". I was told that they had heard that it was seen as an "Inadequate and failing service". It was a shock for me to hear this and started to sow seeds of self-doubt about my ability to manage my new department. But I was not to worry; my new manager would be there to show me a better way of doing things. This was said as a passing comment and very casual, but it did its job. It is why Gas lighting in its smallest form can be very powerful, it can be indirect and you do not always pick up on it straight away.

They say that repetition is the mother of success. Well, when it comes to Gas Lighting repetition for the Narcissist is no different. If you are repeatedly told something on a daily bases and it is reinforced by other facts that are also manufactured, then the manipulation starts to become more powerful.

The level of the gas lighting can often be escalated to greater lengths, for example being promised something and the person later denies all acknowledgement of the promise. I remember being told by my manager "I will email you the link later". When I later asked for the email, they denied that the conversation ever took place. Not just the email, but the whole conversation.

This was then reinforced with the comment "Are you ok, someone else told me you said the same thing to them". So the new manipulated Gas lighting reality starts to take hold.

When the Narcissist is happy that you are starting to doubt your actions, it is a very simple step for them to dig deeper and cause you to doubt your character and identity. For example, "Perhaps this job or industry is not for you" see how they have taken the manipulation to a deeper structure; they are now getting you to question who you are. Again this can often be backed up with a further extended hand of friendship. For example, "I think we should meet for regular sessions, so I can help you out, as you are clearly struggling with this role and I am concerned about your mental health" So once again the Narcissist will put themselves within the role of saviour and create a false co-dependent relationship. This is the part where are you are so vulnerable as you are feeling low, desperate for help and the only person who is extending the hand of friendship is the person who unbeknown to you and everyone else is the cause of your pain and self-doubt. So what do we do in this instance, we gladly take the hand of friendship and think that our problems are now over, but they are about to become much worse.

Finally, the Narcissist has what they want, you crushed not knowing who you are and willing to do whatever the Narcissist says. This is the final stage and you are now in a very vulnerable state and easy to push over the edge.

The tactics are always the same, but the methods are often very variable. It is not just comments that Narcissists make that are used to cause you to doubt yourself. Moving physical objects or completely removing them has often been a popular tactic. The problem with this tactic is that we are so willing to rationalise a situation that we will doubt our own sanity, rather than think that someone is manipulating us.

"I could have sworn I left my keys there, I must be going mad" Does that sound like a familiar sentence and something we all say.

So how do we counter the most powerful technique within the Narcissists playbook? Well, I personally do not believe that it is just enough to be aware, as many people will tell you. There have been times where I believe that we have all been manipulated and were aware of it but still felt powerless to do anything about it. It is a great step to learn how to become more switched on and if you follow the steps I have laid out you will start to see the signs quicker and easier. However you need something more, you need some ammunition of your own.

Now as I have said, dragging a Narcissist into reality is still one of the most powerful techniques you can ever use. Really digging down into the information, for example asking those probing questions "So who said this and how did they know it is the truth?" Never ever let anyone you suspect who is manipulating you off of the hook. The best form of defence in some cases can be a strong attack. Question every single thing that you are told with a counter move. Almost as if you are playing a game of psychological chess, you must always be ready to counter their move and then immediately strike back with one of your own. You should not be argumentative, but calm and rational and totally non-emotional within your responses.

These are some of the counter moves I have used against Narcissists.

Narcissist "You moved my keys again"
Countermove "How do you know it was me"
Narcissist "Because you always do it"
Countermove "Always do it, name 3 times when I have, I want times and dates"

Narcissist "I will send you the email"
Countermove "Ok I will email you now as a reminder of this conversation, so we both remember it clearly"

Narcissist "You are getting very forgetful"
Countermove "No I am not, as I remember you telling me that 3 times in a row now, which means my memory is brilliant"
Narcissist "See what I mean, it's the first time I have ever said that"
Countermove "Actually I think your memory is in question, as I can tell you when and where you said it, do you want times and dates"

What this might cause within a Narcissist is for them to become incredibly annoyed and have an emotional overreaction. They will become agitated and reinforce what they are saying; they may even become verbally aggressive and start shouting, in fact, anything to prove their point. This is nothing more than an attempt to beat you down and resort to a new technique. All that it does is demonstrate that you have a good grip on your mind and sanity and their attempted manipulation has been defeated. Whenever I have counter moved any Narcissist, they have always resorted to shouting, aggression or even more exaggerated lies.

This is a clear sign that you have successfully moved someone into reality and that is a place where Narcissists cannot live or function. If you keep moving them into reality enough, it will start to become uncomfortable for them and they will start to retreat back across the board.

2. The Narcissist Drama Triangle

I first started using the drama triangle when I was training a group of students in how to deal with a crisis negotiation, I had been asked by one of the students if there was a formula which I used, when people were attempting to draw me into the emotions of a negotiation. Narcissists will attempt to draw out your emotions time and time again and this is when their manipulations are more potent. Which is why my mantra has been about remaining non-emotional, staying in reality and being strong-minded.

When I started thinking about writing this book, I was giving a talk on relationships and I introduced the drama triangle into the talk. Someone asked me about Narcissists and it was then that I came up with the Narcissists Drama triangle. So for those of you who are familiar with the Drama Triangle, allow me to show you how the Narcissist plays it.

For those who are not familiar with the drama triangle, it is a social model of destructive behaviour demonstrating a transactional analysis of human reaction to crisis. Or for you non-Social science students, basically it demonstrates the 3 types of behaviour we fall into when a drama occurs and we have to talk to other people.

The classic drama triangle states that when a drama or crisis occurs we will either become a Persecutor/ Accuser, Rescuer or Victim and the behaviours which we will exemplify will fall in line with the role we take on. For example within the classic example between a couple arguing, one may accuse the other of not taking care of the home, pointing out that it is un-kept and dirty. This will result in an interaction where they jump from role to role.

Let's see how this plays out on the Drama Triangle.

The Drama Triangle

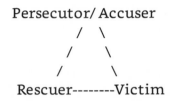

So the couple argue and one accuses the other of not taking care of the home, pointing out that it is un-kept and dirty. The other partner becomes upset and tells them how hard they work, with having to look after the children and also having to work. So the first goes into the Persecutor role, automatically putting the other into the Victim role.

House Mate 1 **Persecutor**:-"The home is dirty, what have you been doing all day"
House Mate 2 **Victim**:- "Do you know how hard I work all day, I never stop"

Now what can happen here is that the Persecutor may then go into the **Rescuer** role "Ok then if it's all too much for you, I will clean the house" This may then cause the other partner to go from **Victim** to **Persecutor** "oh great, so you help out once and that will solve everything" Now the other partner goes into **Victim** role "Oh well I can't win no matter what I do" and so it goes on and on and on.

House Mate 1 **Rescuer**:-"Ok then, if it is all too much for you, I'll do it"

House Mate 2 **Persecutor**:- "So you help out once and think that's enough"

House Mate 1 **Victim**:- "Great I cannot get anything right can I"

Now you may look at these and see them as traditional roles that we all fall into, but if you are a Narcissist then you can cleverly use the Drama triangle as a way to coerce and manipulate someone again and again and again and never let them win. Narcissists will use this technique to wear you down until you are broken and they win.

So let us now take a look at a Narcissist Drama Triangle. When a Narcissist steps up to the drama triangle table they have one of three new roles in mind.

The Narcissist Drama Triangle

Purposeful Persecutor/ Accuser

Manipulative Rescuer-- **False** Victim

Purposeful Persecutor:

They will persecute you with a hidden agenda; this will not be an emotional reaction to a situation, but a planned and staged attack

False Victim: They will portray the victim, to further their agenda, when they are in this role it only serves the purpose of lowering your defences by making you feel bad.

Manipulative Rescuer: They will offer to rescue you, but only to manipulate you and again cause you to lower your defences, this time by appearing to offer a solution. However, this solution will never be delivered.

The other element that the Narcissist will bring to their own drama triangle is that it will always be set up in advance. As I said, theirs will be not be an instant emotional reaction to a set of circumstances, it will have been planned out to the last degree. Unless they just happen upon a drama in which case they will always be ready to jump in and play. Always remember the Narcissist thrives within chaos and drama as they will always be ready to capitalise on it. This is one of the key elements of the Narcissist playbook, to create chaos first and then turn up as the person who can solve it.

So now Let us see the Narcissist Drama Triangle in play.

Narcissist: **Purposeful Persecutor**: "The house is a mess, what have you been doing all day, you know how hard I work all day and I ask for very little in return. It makes me feel awful when I come home and the house looks like this" Intent to make partner feel bad, but not actually improve the house.

House Mate 2: **Victim** "I am sorry, I have been so busy with everything, I just don't know where the time went

Narcissist: **Manipulative Rescuer** "Well if you're not able to cope, I will have to get started on cleaning the house, don't worry, I appreciate that it was too much to ask, to come home too"

Now here is where it will not matter what role you go into, the Narcissist will always be ready for you.

You could continue to be a "**Victim**" and they will verbally berate you more for it while appearing as the "**Rescuer**"

If you became either the "**Persecutor**" or "**Rescuer**", they will easily slip into the "**False Victim**" and you are left with only one outcome

"Feeling bad" about yourself for any of the following:

1. Having been too busy to clean the house
2. Defending your position by looking for sympathy
3. Defending your position to strongly
4. Giving in and then cleaning the house.

Remember with the Narcissist, it is not about how clean the house is, it is about you feeling bad for whatever action you take. So what are you meant to do here?

Winning at the Drama Triangle and the Narcissists Drama Triangle

It is actually very simple; in life when we are faced with impossible situations we only have one choice. Change the game while it is being played. You have heard the saying "A game changer or breaking the rules" This is what you do to defeat the Narcissist on their home territory.

On one occasion I was called to deal with a crisis a man was threatening to jump off of the roof of his building. In his hand, he was carrying a razor blade and he had a large hammer at his feet. He told me if I took a step towards him or tried to talk him out of jumping, he would attack me with the hammer. But he also said that as soon as I left he would slit his wrists and jump. To really test my negotiation skills he finally added that either way he would do one of these, no matter what I did!!!

It felt like I was in a lose, lose, lose scenario. Leave, stay, talk, don't talk I was not going to win here. I knew at this point that it was time to change the game on him. All of the usual things I was trained in were not going to work in this situation. So I calmly looked at him and said "Well what would you do, if you were me, I can't leave, help you or stop you. So what would you do if you were me" He thought about it for a second and laughed and said "You have a problem don't you" I risked smiling back and said "Yeah, I supposed to be doing something, so come on help me out here, I need a new option, how would you handle it?" He thought some more and said "Well you could help me get my telly working again, I am missing Game of Thrones he said and really grinned at me"

I won't go into the rest of the story, but it reached a happy conclusion.

Now I am not saying that you take this approach with Narcissists as it will not work, as the young man on the roof, was not a Narcissist and actually wanted help.

What you need to do, is to not step up to the table, when you do that you cannot play the game. Instead what you are going to create a new role, that of the professional negotiator. You are going to steer clear of blaming, rescuing or being the victim. To do this we are again going to look to our greatest tools, remaining calm, being non-emotional and dealing with reality. Just think about it, if someone wants to play poker with you and the deck is loaded you cannot win. So when they are playing poker, you are going to play chess. You are going to change the game on them. So let me show you how, if we take our last example again, this is a new way of playing it.

Narcissist: **Purposeful Persecuter**: "The house is a mess, what have you been doing all day, you know how hard I work all day and I ask for very little in return. It makes me feel awful when I come home and the house looks like this" Intent to make partner feel bad, but not actually improve the house.

Partner: Yes I can clearly see that the house could do with some work. We both work equally hard and it would be lovely if it looked great every evening. We also both know that it is not just my responsibility, but a joint one. It is not about you asking me to do this; it is about us working together to make it nice

Narcissist: **Manipulative Rescuer** "Well if you're not able to cope, I will have to get started on cleaning the house, don't worry, I appreciate that it was too much to ask, to come home to"

Housemate: "It is not a question of one person not coping; it is about sharing out the duties equally. Shall we sit and draw up a rota that we know we can both stick to?"

Notice the non-emotive reaction this time and looking for mutually agreeable solutions. Now, what does this do to the Narcissistic brain? It will cause it to keep jumping around the table and attempting to play all 3 roles with, itself.

So their next reaction could be:

Narcissist: **False Victim** "You know I work such long hours and my role at work is vital to the company, my job is becoming increasingly stressful and I need my home life to be my sanctuary, it's very little to ask of you"

Housemate: It sound like you need to talk to your manager regarding your work if it is that bad, why you don't make an appointment with them tomorrow. That way you`ll feel less stressed when you tell them how difficult you're finding it. Now let us draw up that rota"

Now the Narcissist can keep on going into whatever role they want, but if you are calmly not playing any of the other roles and being the solution-focused negotiator, eventually you will wear them down. This is one of the great secrets when defeating a Narcissist, you never play their game and if they invite you to play poker, get the chess board out and start making non-emotional moves across the board.

3. Conditioning and committing to the small stuff

During the Vietnam War, many of the US soldiers who were captured underwent a psychological process called conditioning. They were at times treated cruelly by their captors and then treated very well. This threw them off balance and they never knew what the day would hold for them, decent food and rest, or persecution and physical and mental torture. When they were so disorientated that they were ready to break, their captors would sit them in group discussions and discuss the virtues and benefits of Communism with them. They would then have them agree in conversation of how there could be positives of living in Communist society. They would get them to agree to some of the ideologies that Communism advocates, such as everyone being an equal and being treated as such. The kind of things that we would all agree would make the world a better place. Their captors would then record them advocating these statements and then later broadcast them, so people back at home would see them advocating communism and think of them as traitors. Having broadcast the captured troops freely advocating the benefits of a Communism, their captors would inform them that their friends and family back home would be made aware of this and they would be seen as pro-communist sympathisers. They would also inform them that their now former friends, family and unit would despise them for this and disown them. Slowly but surely, the captured troops would feel the distance growing between themselves and their old way of life and friends and look to their captors beliefs as a better way of living and being.

Now if we look at the way Narcissists work they often also employ such tactics to ensure that you are conditioned and committed to their way of thinking whilst separating you from.............yes you guessed it, reality!!!!!

Consider this following example and see what it says to you.

One partner approaches the other one day and says the following to them "When you come in the door from work you have to always come and find me straight away and give me a kiss". If you question that, they may say. "It's a rule of the house and

I like that. If it was questioned further they might say, "Why don't you want to kiss me when you come in". It is a double bind, on the one hand, they have told you that them, wanting you to commit to this action comes from a warm place as they love you. Secondly, they have established it is "A house rule" Thirdly they play their best card, "Don't you want to kiss me when you come in?" If you say "yes", you have bought in" and you can`t say "NO" as they will then act hurt and wounded and make you, feel bad for not following their instructions.

But what happens when they come home from work and you're in the house? Do you think this rule of come and find me goes both ways, of course not.

So consider this, that same person says to their partner "Oh I love it when you greet me at the door when I come home" It`s so nice when you take my bags. "Always do that, always come and greet me at the door I really love it and it tells me that you love me and you know how I sometimes suffer with my back and can`t carry things far" So again, its wrapped in Love "I love it when you do that" They play the second card "It tells me that you love me" so to do it would say that you don't and the ace card, If you don't then your physically hurting me as I have this bad back that comes and goes. So look what they have done, and this is only a really small thing. The minute you're in the house, you're obeying "You have to go and find them, pay homage to them and kiss them" giving them all the power from the second you walk in. And they have set this up so you can't win either way. However, from the minute, their car pulls up you are up out your seat unconsciously thinking if "I don't do this they will think I don't love them" and also if I don't do this it will physically hurt them.

And this is how it starts, this is Narcissistic relationship condition. They will even say things to reinforce what they want like,

"You love it that I want you to come and find me to kiss me the minute I come in". It's a very powerful form of suggestable conditioning. And once they have you committed to the small things and conditioned, it`s so easy for them to just open their narcissistic playbook and decide what is next. They already have you on the small things they can move it up a scale and might say something like "You know I am better with money and dealing with bills than you are" and that reinforcement will be constant. If they win a game of monopoly it's a chance to reinforce and establish their power. They may say, " that is why I hold the purse strings in this family" They will choose emotional moments such as during a game when you have lost to reinforce how much better they are and do it smiling and being silly, so your defences are down and you don't see it coming.

Getting you to commit to the small stuff is the thing that a Narcissist will do, so then you become more complicit and easier to control and they will do this by wrapping their controlling habits in what you perceive as love.

How to break conditioning and committing to someone else's manipulation

Like most of the techniques I have written about in this book, by now you will have started to realise that breaking conditioning involves making sure that you are living in reality, remaining emotionally calm and standing your ground. Now breaking mental conditioning is no different, but it can often be a lot harder to spot. As you can see the conditioning is reframed in a positive manner and you feel that you are definitely doing the right thing and it is good for you. In order to start to see if you are being conditioned you need to do something new; it is a technique that I call, "Going through the Narcissists Looking Glass". You may never have attempted to do this before and if you have not, then it can be quite a powerful thing for freeing and opening your mind, to just what is going on around you. It is actually a really good place to start rebalancing your mind and taking a fresh start at where you are.

To start off with, grab a paper and pen and be prepared to look at your world through a totally different set of eyes.

First I want you to think of a relationship that you are in either your, partner, friend, work or family member. Now answer the below questions in one column and for every question I ask you, I want you to write either Yes or No as you view the relationship.

1. Is there an unequal balance in the decision making in your relationship?
2. Does the other person act more in their own interests?
3. Have you changed for the worse since you have known them?
4. Do you frequently speak negatively of them?
5. Has your financial situation become worse with them?
6. Do they take the lead in the relationship?
7. Do they do most of the talking?
8. Are you doing all the work in the relationship?
9. Does the other person cut you off from others?
10. Do other people tell you this person is bad for you?

Now let us go through the looking glass here. Choose a trusted friend or family member of your and consider how they would answer the same questions about your relationship with the same person. For every question I ask you, I want you to write either Yes or No as you think they would see it.

Now you should have 10 questions and 20 answers. Count the number of Yes`s in the first column and total them up and then take the number of Yes`s within the second column. Then compare them.

Firstly if you have more yes`s than no's in either column, then you need to start to be aware of this persons actions towards you.

Secondly, if you have more yes`s in the first column, ask yourself are you honest with yourself and others about this relationship?

Thirdly if there are more yes`s in the second column then do you need to start to listen to and trust your friends on what they are attempting to tell you?
While this may not immediately solve all of your concerns, what it may well do is get you to open an eye or two and see where others may be taking advantage of you.

Now for the next step in spotting and removing conditioning, we have to reset your mind a little. It is time to go a little deeper here and look into people`s words and the effects that they have on you.

Go back to the last example that I gave you with one partner getting the other to "commit" to two small actions. Notice how they always used a certain persuasive tone and carefully used words such as "You love it when" and "You know" Statements like these are reinforcing statements and can have a powerful effect upon conditioning you, especially when said to you at the right point, such as when hugging you or kissing you, or touching your hand or arm. When someone does this they are anchoring you into a certain way of thinking and associating it with themselves. Narcissists excel at this type of conditioning and anchoring, as it is part of who they are. They will always put themselves in a positive light and getting you to reinforce it at highly emotional moments. This anchoring technique is a key element to look out for if you feel that you are being conditioned into committing to the small stuff. At one point in my career, I had a manager who was brilliant at this and even conditioned my mind into thinking that they always had the answers and were instrumental to my development. They would tell me how they had helped me at key times in my own career progressed, such as when I received positive feedback and would often pat me on the shoulder at the same time.

Think about this, you're positive emotions are running high, you feel great and generous with your thoughts and then someone adds into this feel-good moment, a quick reminder of their brilliance and physically connects with you at the same time. Sound like a familiar scenario to you at all?

So after a fashion, those small suggestions and positive anchor points start to become part of your daily life and before long you are running around committing to large and larger actions and before long, you are doing things to that you would never normally do or put up with and you do not even know why or how you got to this stage. If your friends are totally baffled at just why and how you are putting up with what you do for someone, or why you are behaving so out of character you could very well be in the grip of some very negative conditioning from someone with Narcissistic intent.

Breaking your conditioning

Ok, this is actually easier than a lot of people think, as you were not born to obey Narcissistic people. Your responses to them have been reinforced through manipulation as your conditioning is something that has been done to you by them. Basically, you are just having a response or association to seeing or hearing someone telling you to behave in a certain way. It is nothing more than a Pavlovian response. Pavlov's dogs were taught to drool when he rung a bell as they knew they would be fed soon after the bell was rung. This is not new thinking and it was the first thing I learnt when I studied phycology, for a reason. Pavlovian responses are as powerful and relevant today as they always were. But what we never consider is that Pavlov could have conditioned his dogs to not drool when they heard the bell, he just needed to break their state and give them a new association. Basically, that is what we are doing here, breaking your state, waking you up and giving you some new reactions to Narcissistic abusers. So let us start that process now, this is again a powerful technique that I created and it will free your mind up from just obeying others commands blindly and without thought.

1. Think of the person that you suspect or by now know, is or has conditioned you. To do this make a clear picture of them in your mind as you would see them every day. Now I want you to hear their voice talking to you. Remember what it sounds like.

2. Now I want you to notice the feeling that comes up when you imagine them. Is it fear, tiredness, do you feel sick. Or it could actually be a feeling of excitement of happiness or security. Now, whatever that feeling is, either a negative or disempowering feeling or a positive one, it is the feeling that you are always going into whenever you see or hear them and it is the reason why you have been under their Narcissistic spell. It might surprisingly be a feeling of adulation or even excitement as many Narcissists will generate this feeling and have that Rock Star effect upon others. Whatever it is, you need to change it now.

3. So keep a clear image of them in your head and hear their voice. Now hold that image and sound, but also think back to a time that you were really strong and stood your ground in life. Maybe it was a time when you were calm, in control and were not up for being controlled or manipulated. Put yourself back in that time when you felt great about yourself. Remember what you saw and heard. Now while you are feeling that way, bring back the person to mind who has been controlling you and tell them out loud "NO", say it calmly and clearly and look them in the eye as you are doing it. Then say something like "NO, I will no longer allow this anymore, I am free to make my own choices and they are good choices" Now repeat this action a number of times until you really feel those old feelings of dread or whatever you have been conditioned to feel start to disappear.

4. Now finally to really break your conditioning. Imagine this person looking smaller and weaker in your mind and as you do, continue telling them what you think of them. You can even change their appearance and give them large bunny ears or a clown nose and dress them stupidly, the more ridiculous the better.

5. Now go back to step 3 and go over this process again and again and again, until the very thought of this talking this person makes you feel, strong and in control and really powerful, so the very idea of saying no to them is the easiest thing in the world. What you are doing now is breaking that conditioning and creating some strong neural pathways, so you can gain back control of your mind.

Lesson 5: Going over to the Narc side

Please before you read any further, I know what you are thinking, in this section I am not going to tell you or teach you to be Narcissist, to beat one. No, this section prepares you for the responses that you will get when you are standing up to Narcissist people and how you can counter their counter moves. For you need to always remember when you go up against a Narcissist, it will not just be enough to counterattack one of their moves, they will come back with another. So now let me prepare you for the Narcissist counter attack.

Within my life, I have read two books that I always come back to and they have helped me countless times in all areas of my life. They are amongst the oldest books written and have often been looked upon as some of the first ever books written on strategy and war. They are "The Prince", by Nicolo Machiavelli and "The Art Of War" by Sun Zu. They are still read today by many and I will admit despite only being small in size, they are very hard going. These books have been vital to my learning how to spot and defeat Narcissists and I have based several of my lessons in defeating Narcissists upon the teachings from these books.

Learn to be bad

Machiavelli said, "To be a good leader one must learn to be bad, for it is better to be feared than loved". If ever there was a sentence that applied to understanding Narcissists it is this one. Now let me reinforce something here, I am not saying that you need to be bad or feared, but understanding this teaching will again help you to break free of abuse.

When you get hit by something, or even bitten by something, or you fall over it hurts. We cannot deny that it hurts and we immediately experience that feeling of physical pain, it is not nice and generally, most of us will do whatever we can to avoid it. We are pain averse and quite rightly so. But what is actually worse pain or the sheer unadulterated fear of pain? Throughout my life, I have had all manner of breaks, stabs, thumps and falls that have caused all manner of painful injuries. But not one of them ever prevented me from doing something. However, the fear of pain, be it physical or psychological pain, be it loss or humiliation has caused me to make 10000 wrong decisions based on what others have told me or rather what I have allowed them to plant in my head. Why have I done that? Good old fear as we discussed earlier. These days I am very different and in the words of Gandhi, "I do not allow others to walk through my mind with their dirty feet". When you first attempt to stand up to a Narcissist who is used to having their own way, they will do one of 3 things. They will attempt to manipulate you further; by threatening you with a loss of something they feel you love or need. For example, if you do not do this you will lose your job, money or even there wonderful company. Or they may attempt to hit an emotional hotspot and get upset themselves, they may cry give you a sob story or tell you that others are relying on you. Or they will just threaten you directly. All 3 actions are very powerful as they will put a picture in your mind that this disobedience will result in maybe emotional, financial or even physical pain. This is where Machiavelli really knew his stuff; remember you are dealing with someone who will go to all and any length to manipulate you and the use of fear as a counter move is paramount to them. But how do you counter this, well one way is to target them and not the attack that they are making.

Within the Art of War, Sun Zu said never ever take on an opponent directly, always fight indirectly in an attempt to destabilise them. You can actually use both of these strategies together to stop a Narcissist within their tracks and actually induce a fear-based counter move yourself.

Think of someone in your life who you suspect of manipulating you, what is the worst thing that you could withdraw from them? What is the one thing that may make their life worse if they did not have it? Now here I will tell you one of the greatest hot spots of a Narcissist, which when your hit, will really disrupt their pattern and throw them off balance.

The Denial of omnipotence
When you reframe a Narcissists importance and self-given high status, something will start to go seriously wrong with their already malfunctioning hard wiring. If you start to verbally oppose their grand idealised image of themselves and show them they are not special anymore then you are starting to destructure their self-image. For a Narcissist this is like sweeping a leg or even worse actually seeing the ground fall from beneath them. A former Narcissist who I worked with had a habit of having a qualification for any and every area of life from therapist to space shuttle astronaut they had done it all. They would use these fake qualifications as currency when attempting to override anyone else`s suggestions, which they did for fear of losing face. What made it worse was they attempted to inject fear into others who were also suitably qualified to do so. So after witnessing their attacks several times, I started to see the negative effect that it was having on others emotions and team morale. So the next time they interjected and put others thoughts and

ideas down, I intercepted their attack by de-structuring, not their argument, but the ground that it was stood on. I effectively used the following tool to deny them of their own self-importance.

During one meeting one of the team made a positive suggestion for improvements in the service. The resident Narcissist was straight on it and fearing not being the smartest person in the room shot them and their suggestion down. "Well as you all know I am the solution-focused therapist in the room and I have studied solution-focused therapy, so I have to say that is the wrong route to go and I am surprised that you would make a suggestion like that".

I did not hesitate and jumped in with "Well the good thing is, we are all solution focused here and you don't need a qualification to be able to think that way" They were stunned so I carried on "in fact sometimes being liberated from a specific way of thinking, which we may have gained from a rigid training course can often bring about smarter solutions".

They stopped wide-eyed and I could see them searching every area of their brain for an answer, as if to say "wait a minute, I am not that special" They almost could not speak, which was a relief.

Another time the same person was belittling a member of the team by reminding them that they had had Council social care experience and used to have access to high-level policies and procedures. I stepped in and pointed out that the policies and procedures they talking about were available online to anyone, "even my cat could get hold of them and anyhow they were out of date now", I smiled. Again they did not know where to go and just stormed off, their brain going into meltdown. When you deny a Narcissist of their self-generated importance, it is like taking away their oxygen.

I was once with a partner who asked me if I was attracted to any of the woman on a TV show we used to watch. When I decided to tease her and pointed one out of the woman, she had the vilest reaction to my comments. Not because I had dared to say I found another woman attractive, no her reaction was due to the fact that I pointed out in her words "You cannot find "her" attractive, she is nothing like MEEEEE", she practically screamed at me. An early warning sign of a Narcissist losing her omnipotence which I, unfortunately, failed to spot.

One must learn to be the fox, the lion and the Lamb

Earlier we looked at the pantomime that Narcissists are capable of writing, directing and starring in. Well, now it is time that you learnt to master the 3 greatest roles of your life. Machiavelli wrote that a great leader, must possess the courage of a Lion, be as clever as a Fox and also be able to master the role of the Lamb. You see there are times when the Narcissist in your life will always attempt to reframe you and put you in a role which you are uncomfortable with and at the same time reframe themselves in a positive one. It is a very damaging tactic and can really undermined you and leave them looking like they are your saviour, friend or any other role they choose to put you in. So how do we counter this? Well adopting the mentality of the 3 roles (Fox, Lion and Lamb) or positions is actually a good tactic to adopt. First, you need to be still and cunning like the fox, as when you do this, you are much more aware of what it actually happening around you. To do this you need to need to make sure that you are not always doing all the talking. You need to start listening more to the other side to see what is happening around you. You see you need to spot the snares and carefully avoid them and it is only when you are quiet and listen, that you will spot how and when a Narcissist is attempting to reframe you. So being still and silent at times is vital. Next, you need to have the courage of the lion to the stop them in their tracks. It is all well and good seeing an attack coming, but no good unless you are willing to defend yourself against it. As I say the worst attacks are the ones that I saw coming and choose to ignore. I am not talking about being aggressive here, just remembering that you need to stand your ground and have your say. If you have been in the role of the fox for a while, taking a firm stance will also through them off balance and now they will not see you coming. Finally the lamb, you can always play the open curios and wide-eyed role when dealing with a Narcissist. This is how I perceive Machiavelli's role of the lamb as I will often adopt his more softly approach when dealing with Narcissists. Remember the old saying of soft words strongly spoken can be very effective. You also then do not come across as being over aggressive when you are doing nothing more than defending your position. A well placed, polite, professional and open question that digs down into the Narcissists reframe can piece a hole right through it. So now you are aware of the 3 positions that you need to adopt let us look at how we use them when we are reframed by a Narcissist.

The classic reframe gets a new twist.
We all know now that Narcissists are brilliant at reframing situations to their own advantage. Imagine this, two siblings are sat side by side, (one, happy and successful and the other battling with many demons, in a poor psychological place and envious of their sibling)

A friend asks, "Why are you too so different, one calm and able to deal with the world rationally, the other always so uptight and having to rely on alcohol to get through the day" The one in the poor state of health immediately responds by attacking their sibling "Having to look after them all my life" they say pointing to their sibling. "They have caused me so many problems when I was younger look at me now".

The other sibling who had not spoken just smiled at the friend, they both nodded and the friend smiled knowingly back acknowledging the out and out lie.

Did you see what they attempted there? The unwell, sibling quickly grabbed an opportunity to reframe their own poor responses to the world, put their sibling in the frame of someone who could not cope and put themselves in the role as the courageous hero. This is the classic reframe and your card-carrying Narcissist, carries about a dozen under each arm, one for every occasion.

There is a real problem when you're caught in a reframe; they are hard to get out of. You are boxed in on all sides, so if you cannot break the frame, change the picture inside of it. Now, most people will tell you to reframe the reframe, but with a Narcissist, you are just getting into an attack and defend spiral, no what they will not be expecting is for you to accept their warped version of the truth in a way that totally empowers you. Let me show you.

In the last example, the worst thing for the other sibling to do would have been to have called out the lie, fought against it, or attempted to reframe the reframe. They would have been on the defensive and you never want to be seen to be fighting a defensive game, you just look desperate and guilty.

Here is a great way to change a negative reframe around yourself.
So let us go back to our sibling, they could have said "Yes it is true, I had an interesting background and got into a few scrapes, but I always had the strength and courage to pull myself through them without there being any long term negative effects on my health. I lead a healthy lifestyle and use those experiences in a positive way. I took myself off to college and studied and learnt how to deal with whatever life threw at me positively and I do not blame others. I always take responsibil-

ity for my choices and actions"
Wow, let us break that down.

1. The reframe is acknowledged but within the frame is it called "interesting"
2. The picture is painted as much brighter, "I had strength and courage", "Lead a healthy lifestyle" "used experiences in a positive way"
3. They become the hero of the picture and not the villain "I always take responsibility for my choices and actions"
4. There is also a nod to the poor behaviour of the person attempting to reframe, did you spot it? "I did not blame others"

So the picture itself is changed and the frame remained the same and became of very little importance to the story.

So no matter how many times the sibling came back with the same reframe, they have been drawn out of the picture entirely, the picture that has been painted is a great story where you are able to present yourself however you wish and that is now the main interest.

You will also see the 3 roles that were used here. The Lion, within your own story you stood up to adversity, The Fox, you were smart enough to not overreact to this classic trap and avoided the snare set by a Narcissist and you can even do this in a classic professional and polite manner, portraying all of the attributes of the lamb.

All wars are always won or lost before they are fought.
I was recently asked to be a guest on a radio show and talk about Narcissistic abuse. The presenter asked me about the mind of a Narcissist and how do we ever really stop them. I gave her the answer that I give to so many of my visiting client and that is this. "You may spend a few minutes of your precious time thinking about dealing with a Narcissist person, but for them, it's a full-time job. They live and breathe it 24/7. It is who they are, they do not just go home and hang up their Narcissist cape, and

they are the same at home in the evening. At work, socially it is who they are and always will be. You will never meet and EX Narcissist. When they wake up, it starts again from the minute they open their eyes and they plan every activity through the lens of a Narcissist, every day. As for you, you give it 5 minutes thought before you meet with them. Do you see the advantage they have here?

You need to start thinking of your strategies of how you are going to deal with someone with Narcissistic intent and you need to think not one or two but 20 move`s ahead. Now we all believe that we can create a good strategy, but let me first point out the major thing that most people get wrong when doing this is that they confuse strategy and tactics. Strategy is your long term goal, your end game and if you are going to go up against a Narcissist you are going to need one. If you do not have a strategy for your life, they will have one for you.

For example, your end goal may well be to cut this person out of your life or always be prepared for their manipulations at work. With Strategy, you always work backwards and have an end goal that you need to write down. If I am ever faced with a hostile crisis negotiation, I know my strategy "Preservation of life, ensure that everyone is kept safe and well and everyone goes home that night" However to achieve that strategic outcome I will have to employ various tactics:-

Some of the tactics I use in a crisis situation.
- Research: I will do my research and want to know everything about the situation and the people involved before I pick up the phone.
  - Who is involved
  - What is there background
  - What happened that caused this current situation
  - How many people are involved

- Communication: Establishing communication.
    - what is the best method and route to this
    - What are the barriers to communication
    - Are there any cultural differences I need to be aware of
- Listening: I know how to listen effectively and this will be a major part of what I will do, as listening will enable me to understand what the person really wants.
- Rapport: I will build rapport, so I can gain trust
    - I will employ tactics that allow me to do this
    - Mirroring
    - Paraphrasing
    - Empathetic approach
- Influence: finally I will attempt to influence in a way that will lead to someone changing their behaviour and bring the situation to a positive conclusion.
- Supervision and Support:
    - Is everyone involved ok
    - What do they need now
- Feedback:
    - What could have been done better?

These are only a few of the tactics that I will employ to achieve my strategic outcome. You will also notice that there are even tactics within my tactics regarding communication and rapport.

Also as a footnote, these are not the tactics that I would employ when dealing with a Narcissist, I just wanted to give you an idea of the length of approach that you need to take when you are attempting to really deal with a Narcissist. You already have many tools at our disposal now and it is up to you, to decide how to use them effectively. For example, if you know that you are going to have to deal with someone who makes you feel bad and look bad in front of others you could start by considering what your strategic outcome is? Maybe it is to "walk away from the meeting still feeling good" So to ensure that happened you could use the following tactics

Be good with who you are: Ensure that you reassure yourself so that you are feeling good about who you are. You could use a calming anchor or stepping into to build some self-belief

Focus and Centre: Spend some time before you meet working on yourself. Calm and centre your approach so you do not react emotionally to their words.

Research and Refresh: Go over the section on living in reality and how to move others to it.

Visual reminder: Throughout the meeting have some visual reminders that will anchor you into a positive state, so you remain calm and centred. Write key words down as a code, so you remember your tactics and strategic outcome.

Reframe the drama: As the meeting progresses, have your ammunition lined up, be prepared to play chess when they bluff. Or repaint the picture, if they attempt to reframe you. Use the techniques from section 4 to ensure you are not manipulated or conditioned into any of their Narcissistic plans.

Calm and Centre: Notice your emotions, how are you feeling. Do this throughout the meeting and then when it is over, do it again. On a scale of 1 to 10, how calm are you feeling? Take some time now to do something nice for yourself and do not let any of their words or actions impact upon you.

Appraise: How well did you do? What worked really well for you and what do you need to practise so it goes better next time?

I appreciate that for some people, this may seem excessive just for a meeting. But remember who you are dealing with here. Someone who does not have your interests at heart, is most likely out to harm, ridicule and destroy you at every occasion and take anything and everything they can. When you look at it that way, this is a small amount of planning and preparation which will start to strengthen not only the way that you deal with this person, it will start to strengthen the way you see yourself.

All war is based upon deception

This is one of the most quoted lines from Sun Zu and it is totally applicable to the Narcissistic mind. Of all of the great Narcissistic tactics, I am about to reveal to you the greatest aid to all of their other weapons. This is the stone that sharpens the knife, the laser sight that guides the bullet. It is more than just a case of lying; this is indirect deception on a grand and Narcissistic scale. Consider this, have you ever just suddenly found yourself in a situation that was really wrong or hurtful or even one of total crisis? Have you ever had the rug pulled away from beneath your feet only to reveal there was not even a floor beneath it to land upon? Have you ever just woken up and thought. "How the hell did this happen to me?" or "What happened to get me here?" If you have, I will show you how this happened and how to avoid it happening again.

Some time ago now, I remember waking up with this thought, "How the hell did this happen to me". I woke up with it every day for several weeks, not sure how my life had gotten to such a point of sheer frustration, despair and misery and I did not even know how it got this way. It was almost as if by magic my whole way of life just changed and even when I thought back to the previous 3 months the only answers that I could come up with was, "It was all my own fault and I was to blame" I could not see at that point what had been done to me to cause me such dismay. I felt totally alone in the world and things could not be worse and I was now looking at impending disaster!!!

Now on reflection, none of my thoughts were true as I had been controlled, conditioned and manipulated into thinking this way and it nearly destroyed my sense of self and my emotional health. I just kept thinking "How did this happen, how did it come to this and what had I done wrong to bring this all on myself?" I just could not see how my life had been steered and manoeuvred this way and left me believing it was my fault? Then all of a sudden the answer to it all came in the unusual form of, "Game of Thrones" I had never seen the TV series Game of Thrones so my son bought me the first series as a present to cheer me up. I put it on and I was hooked from the first episode, as I was totally fascinated by the indirect game playing and manipulation from many of the major characters. One thing struck me about Game of Thrones was that anyone who was decent and good appeared to be fair game for the manipulative and Narcissist characters within the show. All of the nice people we rooted for, one by one met their fate. You could almost predict that if someone committed an act of decency, then by the end of the series they would soon be dead. But the other characters who took a more subtler and Machiavellian approach fared much better and for much longer. As I watched the series I saw one by one how some of the more wholesome people found themselves losing their heads "Literally" in some cases and never ever saw it coming. Then it occurred to me when you are dealing with Narcissists they are always indirect within their attacks towards you. It is all about being indirect and using deception. I looked back over my recent experiences with different eyes and ears and suddenly became aware of how blind and indeed deaf I had been. You see most of us are blind to other real intentions and want to think well of them, so on the surface, we believe that all is good. This causes us to follow others blindly, feeling that you are doing the right thing, day in and day out. You do not question others motives and go along with things and then without warning "BANG", your world comes crashing down around your ears and you are left wondering what you did to end up here. You look at yourself and your actions and think "I was good and did as others asked and I have good values and held myself up to them". "I am honest, hardworking and reliable, so why would anyone else be other than the same as me?" But it all still went wrong anyhow. You see our problem is that we assume others carry our good values and this causes us to never look for what is happening beyond the surface, to that all-important deeper level. This is why magicians can get away with what they do. They show us something nice and shiny that keeps us looking in the wrong direction. They point to it and tell us to keep watching it and we do and then suddenly they pull away a scarf and whatever was behind it has disappeared. Such is the way of the Narcissist they are amongst the world's greatest magicians. Take this example to see what I mean. Your partner wakes up one day and without any warning or prior indication tells you "They are not happy as they do not feel as though you have treated them well in your relationship for ages now, almost year in fact, but they choose not to say anything. You feel really bad, apologise and go into overdrive to try and fix things and make it all right again. You do not stop and consider if this is reality or if you are actually to blame. No, you just get to work on your new mission, based on what you have just been told. But the more you try and fix things the worse it seems to get. So you try harder and harder and harder, but nothing works and are told "You are just making it worse" So you try another method and another and another and still cannot get it right. Exhausted and confused you are desperate for guidance and will do or except any help or solution. So you partner sits them down and one Sunday afternoon calmly explains that as they have been so unhappy, due to your behaviour you understand that they have had an affair, but it is ok, as it is over now. You are shell shocked and want to be angry with them for being unfaithful, but now you feel hopelessly lost. Then your partner reminds you, "I was so low and vulnerable due to your behaviour, that I had no choice it was your fault, you did this to us". "What just happened you think, as you are trying to work out how your head ended up on the chopping block. "I destroyed the marriage, I don't remember doing it. I must have done" You get angry, then calm down, then angry again, feel hurt, lost, sad confused and now in a totally bewildered state. Then a little while later, your partner announces. "I am leaving you, due to your behaviour" Stunned and shocked, you replay the last year over and over and can't work out when it began. What went wrong, when did I change and become so bad? Then one morning you wake up alone and think "How the hell did this happen?", and you end up just like Ned Stark in the last episode of series one of Game of Thrones. Not only could Ned he not see what was coming, he could not even work out "How he got there". So you get reflective and looking back over the last year, or 11 episodes in Ned's case and still you do not see it. "How did I get here, you think?", but still, no answers arrive. Actually, you will never ever find out the real answers by asking that question and I will now show and tell you why.

Never ever keep your eye on the ball
Always keep your eye on the ball, that saying is great conventional wisdom isn't it? Keep your eye on the ball, watch the ball, and watch it all the time. Ever seen a con artist playing the old cup and ball con? "Keep your eye on the ball", they say as another person loses yet again. "Keep your eye on the ball", is the biggest myth that is ever been given out to anyone in life. If you want to ever stand a chance of spotting if you're being set up by a Narcissist, then it is time to do something different. Whatever you do, do not ever keep your eye on the ball, especially when people are telling you to. You need to do something totally new, you need to remain aware of the ball, but keep your eye fixed on "The Player"! For the player controls the ball and only they know where the ball is going. The player will reveal the ball's direction every time. But how do we keep our on the player and what do we look out for? Human interaction comes down to 3 things, People, Emotions and Relationships. You could say that most things in life are built on these three components, but how

often do we focus on them? We don't we watch the ball, we see it when it has been kicked and then when it sails by us, we often fail to catch it and some people even get hit in the face with it. We only see the Axe as it is swinging downwards and do not notice how long it took to manoeuvre us up on the platform, get us to kneel down and actually put our head over the basket. It could have taken days, months, weeks even years to get us there, but we only notice the axe when it is falling and why? We do not see it coming because we are distracted by life and whatever those in the world want to hold up to us that is shiny, sparkling, new, exciting or different and as we are watching these wonderful things, we are missing what is really happening. We allow ourselves to get so wrapped up in our work, TV, the internet, social media and everything else, that we miss what is really happening. Guess what, Narcissists don't miss a thing, they notice everything and realise that in life there is a game within a game, a metagame if you like. A secret game of indirect deception and they know how to keep you from knowing that this game even exists. So now let me introduce you to this game within the game, so you can learn how to extract yourself from it.

People, Emotions and Relationships

By now we are really getting under the skin of the Narcissist and hopefully, you have a sharper eye on what is actually going on around you. But I want to take that to an even deeper level now, by teaching you how to see what is really happening around you and to do this we need to learn even more about observing, people, emotions and relationships.

People

It does not matter what you do in life, IT, health, security, finance, service, law, science, entertainment. Every job comes down to people and learning how to be more aware of them. While I have been writing this book, I have still held down several other roles and run my businesses. Now as varied as all of my businesses are, they all are, they all rely on people skills. You can never ever lock yourself away from other people and the more you do the bigger target you become. Narcissists although self-absorbed, are often brilliant observers' of human behaviour. You will normally find Narcissists right in the middle of human interaction, making themselves relevant to others, by telling them how they can meet their needs. Let us go back to Game of Thrones again and look at another interesting character. Tyrion Lannister is without a doubt one of the most interesting characters within the series, he is the least physically capable of all of the characters and in this cut-throat world, you would think that would make him the most vulnerable. But he has survived every major cull, military coup and clever manipulation thrown at him. How does he do this while kings, warriors and wise men and woman all around him fail and falter? Easy, he pays attention to people and takes an interest in what they want. I have lost track of how many times I have heard him ask of others a fundamentally important question that no one else ever bothers with "What do you want? What do you want?" is really important, not just the question but the mindset itself. We spend most of our time, focusing on ourselves and what we want, that we never think of what others want. To be better prepared to notice what is going on around you, you need to start paying a lot more attention to other people. You will always find that people are only too happy to talk about themselves, especially Narcissists. Now while we cannot actually rely on the answers that they are giving us as truthful, it does give us an opportunity to get them to reveal more about themselves. Some people with Narcissistic intent could talk about themselves all day and all night and probably never ever pause for breath. Now if you are centred and able to listen carefully to them, they will give you clues to their intentions and how they operate. For example, if I had been more astute years ago when I was in the company of someone who told me they had "dated tradespeople to get free work done" then I may have saved myself a lot of heartache later on. When you are listening to someone, do not just listen to the words, notice the passions that arise within them and listen to their story. Really listen and think what this tells you about them. You can never be 100%, but it can help to build a picture. People will love to tell you their story when they do listen to them. What you are attempting to do here is build up what is called your sensory acuity. You are listening more to the ideas and concepts behind what people are telling you. Doing this will start to get you into the habit of examining behaviour and questioning it and not just accepting it. Why did someone who you hardly know, unexpectedly just turn up to your house with coffee? Do they like your company? Do they want to get in your house to take a look around? Do they want to feed you information while you in your own home, relaxed and calm? They are smiling and that coffee smells great, always question peoples motives.

Emotions

You may be feeling that at this point you cannot listen to any more about emotions at this time, or you may be feeling great and happy to learn more about how you can feel stronger and more assured. Now read that last paragraph again and notice what I did with my words. I used my words to affect your emotions. ("You may be feeling great and happy" and "you can feel stronger and more assured"). We are emotionally based units that can be lead around blindly in life as long as we are happy with what is happening, or what we feel is or will be happening. When you have a date, you feel excited about it, right up to the point where they cancel, then you feel disappointed and are slightly vulnerable and might do something to create that feel good emotion again until the sad feeling goes away. Ever fallen into that trap on a Friday night? Have you ever ate or drank out of boredom or sadness? yes, well that is your emotions acting up.

So imagine this, If I could engage your positive happy emotions, or your negative fearful emotions every time we met I could just perform the most amazing diversionary sleight of hand right under your nose as I would be keeping you in either a high or low emotional state, just imagine what I could get away with if I did that to you every time we met? To keep you in the dark and away from their real intentions most Narcissists will always be attempting to engage the emotions of love, fear, happiness, guilt, shame, or whatever they see as best to manipulate you for the time. They will use stories to manipulate you. We all love a good story as we have learnt from childhood that story's teach us important lessons and mostly the stories we grew up with are about tales of good morality that teach us how to be decent. The one thing a Narcissist will do is use a tale of morality to make you believe that you are the one out of integrity. They will use words that incite hatred, anger or fear to press your buttons. They will shout and use volume, as we are born with a fear of loud noises. They will talk in an over-dramatized manner and some days it is like being around a great actor in full flow. They will use these emotional buttons pressing tactics when they want to incite you to bend to their will. In fact, they will use any tactic that effects your emotions to keep you away from seeing what they are really doing. You see as humans we are programmed to respond to our emotions, so guess what when someone has a way of pressing our buttons, their tactics always work. Advertisers, Politicians, Religion and Mass Media have been engaging our high and low emotions forever and it works, without fail. The cover of this book has a happy smiling face being pulled away with a very different one behind it, that image could capture my point. We see someone smiling at us and we smile back and then feel good, we relax as our happy emotions are engaged and then without warning before we know it, they pull off the mask and our head is over the basket.

So just start to be aware of the power of others words and actions upon your emotions, sometimes we all need reassurance and want to feel nice about ourselves, it is seductive to listen to the words others may tell us, however, these words can easily cause us to just close our eyes and blindly follow.

One of the greatest tricks of the Narcissist when attempting to engage our emotions is offering us what we most desire they will offer us, love, wealth, company, stability. When we first meet a Narcissist they will question you and find your needs and wants and they will do it simply by asking "What do you want". Then when they have found your heart's desire, they will match your needs to what they claim they can offer you. Now you are vulnerable with your emotions fully engaged in this way and promises of your desires about to be delivered, why wouldn`t you just close your eyes and happily drift off into a fantasy world of their making. So how do we stop this very powerful diversionary technique and prevent ourselves from just being lead around by our emotions?

Stop, stop and just centre and wake up.
So just stop, stop right there and slow down, the reason why I always say this that we need to keep centred and emotionally balanced is for this very reason. I never let anyone capsize my boat ever. It is firmly anchored to the rocks these days. Emotive words, when mixed with great intonation of voice and a promise of what might be can sway people to all manner of actions, both through fear and love; but only if you allow them to. If ever you feel that you are about to take action from high or low emotion, stop and think about what you are doing. There is a reason why I wrote a chapter saying wake up and smell the Narcissist. Whenever I am working with a client if they are going too far down a negative route, I will break their state in a session and ask them, "Can you smell coffee"? Whatever they were thinking, they will usually stop and attempt to engage this new sense and it will stop them dead in their tracks. It will drag them from their negative emotions and bring them back to..............you got it, reality. I want you to start stopping, then waking up and being centred. Whenever you feel that you are being coerced or manipulated as your emotions are being

fed either good or bad feelings, then just stop and ask yourself a question that will break your emotional state. Or actually, take a moment, put your hand up and say "I need a coffee here and to take a moment alone, before I agree to anything" Hit the pause button and do not let anyone convince you that your decision is time limited. Then actually go away and think about what you are being asked to do, or agree to. Is this something that makes sense in your head, or are your emotional buttons just being pressed? You need to separate the two right now so you will then become aware of what you are being asked to do, or led into. You have to ask "is right for you?". This may just sound like common sense, I know. But when dealing with Narcissists, they drag us off our common sense ground and take us into their distortions. This is how we get back to our own non-emotional reality, with some grounded rational thought. Notice if you do this and take time over your answer, how do they respond? Are they happy that you have done this, or are they pressuring you into making snap decisions?

So, now you are becoming more aware of people, their actions and their words and how they can affect your emotional decision making, now let us move to the final part of the trilogy, relationships

Relationships

Remember the moment in the movie "Love Actually" when during a press conference, Hugh Grant stands up to the President of the United States of America. He starts off responding to the Presidents remark about "Our Special Relationship, being still as special as ever", by saying "I love that word Relationship; it covers all manner of sins doesn't it". You know what, he is correct as the bullying and manipulative President uses his power within the "relationship" in the movie to act in a manner which is borderline Narcissistic. He takes what he wants, gives nothing back and as is said within the movie, "casually ignores all of those things that are important to others". He then stands and smiles before the world and boasts how great the relationship is. Is any of this sounding familiar to you? Even the word "relationship" can be used like a stealth warplane in full flight to bomb you into total submission and ensure that you do not even think about raising your head and disagreeing.

Just read these following sentences.

"But it is important to our relationship that this happens"
"In any good relationship that is just what the other person does"
"That is what I am aiming for in our relationship"
"This is the only way our relationship can continue"
"You saying that means that our relationship is not important to you"
"But we are in a relationship here so we need to do that"
"This is more important, it is about our relationship"

I could go on and on and on and give you 100 other sentences that all have the same intent, to get you to do what the other person wants, for the good of "Your relationship". Those sentences are powerful sentences and whenever you hear one, you need to stop and think. The "R" word whenever it is used in any sentence by someone who is attempting to get their way is very dangerous indeed. So let us look at why it is the Narcissists favourite part of the playground to take you to.

Why the Narcissist loves Our Relationship
The term relationship is such a powerful word, isn't it? It is a classic reinforcing and connecting word. It signifies a unification of some sort and sense of belonging and being part of something and as humans, we like that. Being in a relationship is seen as a good thing and mostly we want to stay in one, as the opposite of being "In a relationship" is being "Out of a relationship" Notice how these sentences sound and make you feel"
"I am in a relationship"
"I have started a new relationship"
"Our relationship is just beginning"

Now notice how these sentences make you feel. They are all positive and feel good words that we like to tell people about and they make us feel nice.

Now read the following sentences

"My relationship has ended"
"My relationship is over"
"Our relationship has come to an end"

They make you feel sad and all signify something bad in your life. It is a disturbing fact that Narcissists have the ability to control and manipulate people into actually wanting to stay in a bad or abusive relationship. The reason they can do is that it is easy to get others into thinking that the alternative (being single, alone, or out of or not in a relationship) is worse. We are not solitary creatures and we look to develop relationships with others, it is what we do and this is a good thing. The problems arise when we want to be in any relationship in or stay in one no matter how bad it is, rather than be out of one. This is gold dust to a Narcissist and the dependent relationship is the jewel in their Narcissistic crown. A relationship is their end game, their final solution and all their cruel and harmful tactics are aimed at achieving this final strategic goal, a relationship with you. But not a good relationship, they want to create one that you do not feel that you can leave, as even though life is bad for you in this relationship, they want you to think that life will be worse out of this relationship.

At one time in my life, being out of a certain relationship filled me with fear and dread. Where would I live, what would I do every night after work, who would I be without my "RELA-TIONSHIP". But it is not just the romantic relationship we fear losing. What about our "Work relationships, our friendships our family relationships" Again we are back to those perceived feelings of lose and pain if they fall apart. The Narcissist mind

143

knows of the real power of "Our relationship" and will use it to batter your senseless. Have you ever had someone threaten to end your relationship, no matter what type it was? How did it make you feel and what did you do to attempt to make sure that it did not happen? This is where we really need again to go through that looking glass and start to see ourselves differently.

Never ever be attached to the outcome.
This final piece of Narcissistic thinking is actually one that I discovered quite by chance when I was out in a bar with a friend one evening. The friend, in particular, was discussing attraction strategies and how we approach people when we are out. They admitted that one of the things they had always admired is someone who can walk up to a complete stranger in a bar or club and start talking to them with a view to getting to know them better; a sort of cold calling approach if you like. Now whether it is just who I am, or years having to make potential cold leads when I worked in the corporate world, or whether I am just able to build a relationship and empathy really quickly I don't know. Whatever it is, I am really happy to just approach total strangers and talk to them no matter what the situation. When I discussed this with my friend, they mused over it for a while and said it was because I had no anticipation of either a positive outcome or a fear of a negative outcome. Thinking about it, they are correct as I do not focus on a negative or even a positive before I approach someone; so I feel really comfortable about making contact. My philosophy here is "the only outcome that I get will be the one that I get". The only thing that I do know with some degree of certainty is that if I do not approach anyone, either for business or to make friends then the chances are reduced of anything happening, which is just a fact. It is the same reason that I am happy to give public talks; I do not have a perceived idea of how they will go, so I do not attach any emotions either good or bad to them. I know what I want to say and I am happy to answer any questions, full stop.

So what has this got to do with Narcissistic thinking? Well, I am certain that I do not possess the mind of a Narcissist, for one thing, I genuinely care about other people and I can empathise with them. I would never approach someone if I felt that I would intimidate them or make them feel uncomfortable. This is one of the main things which set`s us aside from Narcissists. When a Narcissist approaches someone with a view to committing all manner of dreadful atrocities they are totally unattached to any emotional outcomes of the encounter, which either they or you may have. They just know that whatever act they are planning on committing, will quite possibly get them what they want and remember that is their only priority is self-gratification. When we plan to commit an act we will think through the elements of risk and harm to ourselves and others. We may be happy to approach someone and ask them to help us with something; however, we will be mindful if there is any level of risk or harm and if there is we will change our plans or, not approach them. Not being attached to the outcome for me does not mean that I am boundaryless; it basically means that I am personally ok with a yes or no answer as I have a good sense of self-worth. The Narcissistic brain is different, it will just have an idea of what the outcome will be for themselves and not just care of the effects of achieving it will have on anyone else.

This is an area of Narcissistic thinking that we need to be aware of this, as when they approach out of nowhere with this non-empathetic cold calling approach we can often be blindsided and taken in by what we see as their incredible self-confidence. Now a person can approach us in such a manner and if their intentions are good, then it is up to us to allow ourselves as to whether we wish to go with what they ask. However, we have to be on our guard with all cold callers, as we have no idea what their intent is. The best way in which we can always protect ourselves here is by either drilling down by questioning into what it is that they want, or by giving them a very definite "No".

Always remember that a Narcissist hates the word "No" and will also struggle when you wish to drill down into their request for you to do something. As they are not attached to the emotional outcome, they may very well struggle to give you a definite answer as to why you should do what they want and become very upset with you even questioning them. This is because you are making that all-important challenge to their already damaged ego and perceived sense of superior self. They just cannot stand to be questioned and remember once more you are dragging them into reality with your questioning.

How to not be attached to the outcome of other words

If ever you think this is the case and you are being cold called by a Narcissist then you need to counteract this behaviour by mirroring them and also not being attached to the outcome yourself. This mindset is actually much easier than you realise and one that is great to adopt when dealing with Narcissistic people. The best way to adopt a "not being attached to the outcome mindset" is by thinking of a situation this way. A moment ago your life was as it was, neither good nor bad, it just was. Then someone then came along and painted a picture for you that predicted either disaster or great fortune. They said some words which caused you to create some artificial pictures in your head and they also attached a meaning to those pictures that created pain or happiness. Now your emotions are fully engaged and they have you off and running in whatever direction they wish. You are either seeing doing what they want you to do as making your life great if you do it, or seeing your life as getting worse if you do not. You are now attached to the outcome, but remember it is their outcome and not yours they have just put it in your mind. Ok now stop, freeze all the pictures in your mind and blank them out, turn the volume down on whatever it is that you are telling yourself. Basically, clear your mind for a second. Now notice what feelings you had, if they were excitement or fear this is what button was being pressed. Now think again about what you have just been asked to do, just think about the words and make no pictures. Do you still want to do this, from a calm and non-emotional point of view? You are no longer attached to the outcome emotionally and need to apply cold hard logic to the situation.

It is often the case that we can easily do this to ourselves as the pictures and words we choose to make in our mind ourselves prevent us from taking action. You need to practise doing this, take back control of the pictures and sounds in your mind and see what you are being asked to do from a cold and logical point of view.

5.VERBAL JUJITSU

The following chapter is something that you really need to study and work on. It is helpful for dealing with those narcissistic people who you just have to deal with every day, either in your work or within your family or circle. It is something that I have studied and researched and I have called it verbal Ju-jitsu. Ju-jitsu is a martial art that allows you to use other peoples strength against them. Now while I have covered how to verbally assert yourself with Narcissists in Chapter 4, I wanted to give you some more ammunition on the verbal battleground, as that is where the Narcissist can often be the most effective within their manipulations. So read, study and practise the following when you have to take on someone who attempts to verbally manipulate you.

1. Do your research

Yes, it is boring and dull, but it can really give you an advantage when you turn up and not only know the facts of whatever you are discussing but the opponents side as well. Always play the other sides hand here and think, what are they going to bring up and discuss and what will they be researching? Know your subject inside out, because if you do not then your opponent can tell you whatever they want (Narcissists inevitably will) and they will say it with such conviction that even you will believe what they bring to the argument or discussion. Remember to call them out on their facts, if it is important to what is being discussed. Do not let them get away with just stating anything in order to claim a victory.

2. Spot paper brick wall arguments

Narcissists have a habit when you are verbally fencing with them of what I call throwing up a paper brick wall. From the front, the brick wall looks solid and impenetrable, but when you look at it from a different perspective, it is just paper thin. For example just because someone tells you that 8 out of 10 people prefer someone it still does not prove a point. This is the classic "wisdom of the masses" argument as I have coined it. I have seen it so many times and while it looks convincing it is not a reason to go along with someone`s thoughts or change your mind over your ideas. For example, I was once given the following argument by a colleague with highly narcissistic tendencies.

"Everyone agrees that this is the way it should be done and it's the only fair way of doing it. If most people want this, then that is what should happen"
Now read that statement again, there is not one single solid argument there. All of the points were paper thin. Their argument hung on this formula:-

Everyone agrees + Should be done + Only fair = Do what I say and what I want

Just look at their points and the language they have used, it is the argument of the manipulative in full flight. The words everyone, should and fair. These are total non-arguments and you are allowed to and should disagree with all of them.

Your response should be to break that argument down into its separate components and deal with them individually.

Everyone: it might not be everyone's decision to make, only yours
Should: Always turn that word should, into could, as it gives your flexibility
Fair: This is a word that implies to do something this way is right. Fair for who? usually, the person manipulating you.

See how their argument falls apart when torn down, always take time to deconstruct a paper brick wall and never be afraid to just disagree with them.

Also, someone could easily bring in the name of a heavyweight to reinforce their argument and you are allowed to disagree with them as well, it does not matter who they use to reinforce their argument.

I once had someone tell me that their idea was backed up by the head of the local council. I calmly told them, "I can also disagree with the head of the local council as well and that I did not have to agree with someone just because of a title or a position". All that proved was that the head of the local council agreed with them, it still did not mean that I had to agree. You are allowed to disagree with people who have status; remember many well-known people in life have made bad decisions. Do not let Narcissist people clamber onto the shoulders of giants to reinforce their arguments.

3. You have offended me

So what, be offended in the words of the great stand-up comedian Steve Hughes "Be offended, nothing happens. Being offended is subjective". The "you have offended me" argument is an emotional response that attempts to sway you to changing your mind. The Narcissist mentality is so in tune with the "You have offended me mentality" in order to win that they will play the hurt and upset card time and time again. Let them be offended, you can tell them you are sorry that they are offended and upset, that was not your intention, but your argument still stands and you sticking to your guns. Let them be offended if that is what they are claiming. They will not die from being offended and it will show up their Narcissistic behaviour for what it is. We do not go out to deliberately hurt and upset others and apologies if we do, but it does not change our minds when someone attempts to manipulate us by saying they are offended. You are allowed to disagree with someone and if they cannot accept this calmly and rationally, be aware.

4. Non-emotional reaction
This is where all of our efforts of being focused and using meditation comes into play. Never let others push your emotional buttons in order to draw you into action. As the minute you start to react emotionally, you have lost and your opponent has won. Remain calm throughout the whole interaction and you will have greater control over your reactions and not just agree to others wants and needs.

4. Question and drill down into their arguments
Never let anyone get away with a generalisation within an argument. If someone tells you that something you have said or done is wrong, ask them why it is wrong. Do not allow them to drag you into their reality distortion field. Get them to be specific and justify their comments and do not let them get away with the "Well that is what everyone does". I have for a number of years known someone who will to this day talk in generalised statements and arguments with no substance to back it up. They will often throw out at another person "That is terrible, you should not do that, or they were awful" but have no real intelligent or tangible structure to the argument. Just getting them to drill down into each statement, quickly shows it up for what it is.

To respond to this, never ever defend their generalised statements, drill down first and get them to be more specific, drag them into reality.

5. Look out for Back door arguments and Trojan horses hidden within those arguments.
Always look out for anything that is snuck in through the backdoor within an argument. This is another major distortion and Narcissists love to introduce these points almost within a further wooden horse. I once worked with someone who would link up very contentious points with whatever argument they

were attempting to sway people with and embed further negatives within that. For example, I remember them sneaking their point about a new style of supervision that other managers were looking at as "an unsafe practice". After the first time they embedded their argument within their opening remarks they would only refer to this style of supervision as "This unsafe practice, or within a few sentences "Very unsafe practise". After a while, they casually "Remarked that this very unsafe and "time-consuming" style of supervision does go against modern HR practices. The sentence was used so many times by other people around the table, that they easily had everyone scrap this supervision. No one wanted an unsafe practice within the company, but the real coercion was the "Time consuming" comment. Not one manager wanted a more time consuming practise put in place. On reflection the other style of supervision was not unsafe, it was different and a more positive style of supervision, but it was not a style this person wanted or agreed with. They wanted to keep the style they had created which battered staff over the head for not working hard enough.

Over the years as a therapist, I have met with so many people who hold a poor opinion of themselves as the abusive person with who they are in a relationship with has constantly linked their sense of self-worth to something negative and they are not even aware of and then buried further negative arguments within their comments. It is the same for those who always give you nicknames and reinforce certain hidden ideas about you whenever you get into a discussion with them. For example "Here you go being over sensitive again and panicking everyone with your inability to be strong". Look how many negatives they have packed into that sentence alone.

Of all of the arguments that someone will present, this is one of the hardest to counter, as we will not be able to see it coming and when we do, it is hard to see how they made the assumptions in the first place, which actually makes it harder to disagree with. I will show you how it works if someone saw a movie that you had not and came back and told you that the film was terrible. It would be hard for you to defend the film, as you had not seen it as you are not aware of how they built their arguments. So they could point out all the reasons that the film is bad. They could tell you the following "The cinema was empty no one laughed at the jokes and people walked out". Now on that basis, you may not go and see it due to all their negative comments. So you are now making a decision on the arguments within the narrative. But you might think, if you did go and watch the film, you might actually enjoy as it had good reviews. However if someone told you that the heating in the cinema was broken where it was showing and it was cold and also you could hardly see the film as it was dark and come to think of it, the sound was muffled. They may then tell you that their car was vandalised when they came out, as it is only showing late at night. Now you may really think twice about going. For a start the film according to them is no good, but hidden within the argument is the fact that it is no longer the film that is no good, it is now an unpleasant or even dangerous experience to even go and see it. This is classically how a Narcissist will win their arguments with you, they will sneak an argument in the back door and hide a further argument within that and totally change the narrative on the argument and you.

So just how we deal with this? The main problem with this deception is that we have a negative buried within a negative and even if we deal with one hidden negative we have the other one to deal with. So we are constantly on the defensive, which is not great ground to be on. Now we could deal with the negatives point by point as we have done with paper brick walls. Or we could play the Narcissist at their own game and reframe every one of their own arguments as a positive. However, I have another much more effective way of dealing with this strategy.

I once had a client, who was a young and successful in many

aspects of their lives, but they had suffered at the hands of some Narcissistic people who had left them with an anxiety around social situations. They were popular and people liked them, but they had become too guarded and would not attend social functions due to the feelings that they generated in them. After a number of weeks, we started to build a tactic that would allow them to become more comfortable about being in other peoples company whilst still feeling safe and protected. I ended up calling this tactic the Drawbridge and Portcullis. Many years ago during feudal times, Castles had a drawbridge that usually was lowered over a moat. When it was raised access to the castle was very difficult. However when it was lowered anyone could get in and were free to access the inner areas of the castle. However some castles had a second line of defence a Portcullis, this was a heavy iron gate that was dropped and prevented anyone gaining accesses to the castle even if the drawbridge was down. It had the added advantage that you could still see your enemies through it and even communicate if you wished, all from a position of safety. Now when dealing with Narcissists who are attempting to use deeply embedded deceptions within their language this tactic and mindset is ideal, as it allows you to safely engage with people but does not allow their deceptions or negativity in.

So whenever you think that someone is attempting to subvert a negative argument in and then even embed a further negative within that, this is what you do.

1. Lower the Drawbridge and invite them across it. To do this first openly engage them in a positive discussion regarding their comments. Use open questions, for example, tell me more about your thoughts, go with the Mediators favourite 4 W`s and a H (when, what, where who and how)

But whatever you do, do not at any point look to agree with any of their comments. You are merely inviting them across the drawbridge to talk so you can listen. Also, do not let anything they say affect you emotionally. Remember you have your Portcullis down so their words will not have any effect on you. At this stage, you are just information gathering.

2. Keep your Portcullis down, and respond from a position of safety. Reflect back to them everything that they have just said and ask them if you have understood them correctly, (Factually correct) and do they have solid evidence to back it up. Still, do not agree with anything they have said and remain in a non-emotional state, this also includes not responding to humour, aggression, guilt or humiliation.

3. Refuse to accept the Trojan horse. Now the story of Troy would have been very different had they had just refused to accept the gift of the wooden or Trojan horse. Imagine it, "We have this great gift for you as a peace offering, could you just open the gates so we can wheel it in?" "Erm no it is ok, we can see it from here, we appreciate your efforts and we are happy to talk peace, but the horse would not really go with the décor, besides It is huge, where would we put it? The Trojan horse was it only effective when it was allowed into the walled city and the Greek soldiers hidden inside were able to attack from the inside under the cover of darkness. This is the same as the verbal Trojan attack that Narcissists will launch upon you. It will seem as though they are telling you something for your own good, but as soon as you accept it into your head and respond to it, they are able to do the most damage. To refuse a Trojan horse the best defence is to refuse the idea that you are being sold. Not outrightly disagreeing, but stating that the thoughts or experiences of the other person, from your perspective, experience, and viewpoint just do not work for you. Just think what that does to their brain!!! You have just refused their gift, not outwardly told them they are wrong, just refused to accept this "Helpful" information. So now they are standing on your drawbridge and have to pull this huge Trojan horse back across it. They may try again and represent it to you maybe they have painted it a different colour, or put wheels on it. But it is still not something that you have to accept. I have seen many a Narcissist search every area of their brain when I have refused to accept their gift of lies and manipulation. It usually results in them becoming either aggressive, reinforce the negatives of what they are saying or add new elements to their manipulations, "They are totally Machiavellian, you need to be careful of them, I am only warning you for your own good" were the words of a Narcissistic manager who was attempting to destroy the credibility of a member of my team I had yet to meet. I acknowledged their thoughts but said "I will wait until we meet in person so I can hear their thoughts on the situation" I did not agree with anything they said or even nodded. They nearly burst a blood vessel and then went into a 30-minute rant on the person, which told me who the Narcissist was from the outset.

Always remember, just because someone tells you something with total conviction that they swear is genuine and is for your own good, you do not have to just eagerly nod, lower the Drawbridge, raise the Portcullis and invite this thought in. It is nothing more than a thought within their heads, which they are attempting to plant in yours.

6. KNOW THE NARCISSIST IN YOUR LIFE

1. The Narcissist Partner

There are usually two types of Narcissist which we end up getting into relationships with. Firstly there are those Narcissists who find us when we are low and promise to give us what we want, then take it away and give it back, then take it away again. They play that classic give and take game and we never really know where we are with them. They confuse us so much that we end up not even sure if we are actually in a relationship with them or not/ They totally confuse us until that our sense of reality becomes distorted beyond belief. They come and stay for a while, usually taking whatever they want and give back very little even their time. They leave you feeling empty, uncertain and abused. If we open our eyes and our ears to our real friend's comments then it is very easy to spot these people. We can actually get these Narcissistic people out of our lives really quickly. When we do, we then need to get back our sense of self and wellbeing and use the time they are out of our lives to heal and see them for who they are and the damage they are doing to us.

The second sort of Narcissist that we end up in a relationship with, are far more dangerous and very difficult to remove from our lives. They fall into the category of the covert Narcissist and like a sleeper terrorist cell can hide themselves away for years, unless you know what you are looking for. They can cause the most damages as they spread their Narcissistic tendrils into every area of our lives. They infiltrate our thoughts on friends, families even our work and who we are for such a long period that their way of thinking becomes the norm. We do not see it, as they are masters of their art and know how to press our emotional buttons. We share everything with them and give up our secrets, feeling that we have found someone we can totally trust, who will never hurt us. They will even tell us this "I would never do anything to hurt you". Then one day without warning, we see them without their mask on and it hits you like a fast-moving train. You are living with, have married, or are in a long term relationship with a complete Narcissist!!! You need to be really careful with relationships, any relationships that you enter into. Do you know who you are starting to get involved with? We just do not stop and think about it and get carried away with our emotions. One of the best ways to spot a narcissist early on within a relationship is with the "No" test. Say "No" to them and see how they react to this. Do they say "Ok and shrug their shoulders" or does the very idea that they are not going to get their way infuriate them. If they are hiding, then they may actually take the Narcissists clever third option and agree, but then immediately attempt to influence you into their decision they have just suggested.

By now, you will be aware of all of their clever ways to manipulate you and how you can make a counter move around their manipulations. The "No" test is always quite effective in rooting out potential trouble. The other thing to be aware of when you are in a relationship with someone who you suspect has Narcissistic tendencies, is the hard and soft selling technique. This can often be something that attracts us to certain people; they can initially appear charismatic on the surface and get away with all sort of behaviour, through the use of their charming personality and selling others their ideas with stories and tales that bring down others defences. But if you are in a relationship, they should not be doing this with you? If your partner is forever still selling you, then this is a huge red flag that they are not authentic and genuine. A mature grown-up relationship is where two people talk and listen and support each other. They work together over shared goals and plans and are able to tell the other if something is not working. If your partner is forever "Selling you concepts, dream and ideas", either by playing to your emotions or with veiled threats or acting hurt if you are not sold on their idea then something is not right.

The Narcissist Boss

This is one that we may all have experienced for one very good reason, Narcissistic people love to climb the ladder and obtain positions of power. If you read back to my section on "How a Narcissistic brain works" then you will see that to hold a position of power, "a legitimate power" over others is nothing short of an aphrodisiac for a Narcissist. But how do you know if your boss is a Narcissist or, someone who just you do not like? We have to be careful here as it is far too easy to categorise our Manager as a vile evil and manipulative Narcissist, just because you do not like the way they conduct themselves at work. I once worked for someone who`s behaviour at times some people might describe as appalling regarding the way they presented themselves. I mean behaviour that would now have many people raising an eyebrow and picking up the phone to the HR department. But the one thing they were not was Narcissistic, they displayed not one Narcissistic trait, but believe me it would have been easy to call them out as one. We need to be careful here as raw naked ambition is not always Narcissism either. I have worked for and with highly ambitious people, who wanted to improve a service and themselves in the process, but this was also not Narcissism. There are times when we all need a bit of an ego to be able to push ourselves forward in life. Those Managers, who can lead a team, will need a good strong ego and high levels of self-belief in order to see their vision become a reality. That is also not Narcissism.

No, what we are looking for is total office game playing. Underhand, double-dealing, idea stealing, false friend making, lying, self-proclaiming, ranting, swearing and shouting Narcissistic

Management. I first discovered the ideal way of spotting a Narcissistic manager after they "left" a company I was working for. I sat down with one of my work colleagues and they calmly said to me "They only have one style of management and that style is dividing and conquering the team" That sentence pretty much just states the only strategy Narcissistic Managers have and any of the tactics they employ will have the end game of dividing others. For the Narcissistic boss knows, if you can keep everyone off balance, looking over their shoulders and not trusting each other, then you can create chaos in a person's mind. Now when someone is in that chaotic and paranoid state, who do they turn to for friendly help and support? Yes, you guessed it, the friendly always helpful and on hand Narcissistic manager. For example, look at the Trojan Horse strategy, they will tell you something behind closed doors that only you are privy to and you are not to tell anyone else. They will give you this great gift and if you accept it and allow it to infect your thoughts and minds, then they have you. So you then start behaving differently towards your colleagues due to what you have been told. Your colleagues will notice this change in you, but your Narcissistic manager will have also had a similar conversation with them about you. So they will see your new behaviour through this negative filter your manager has given them. Now you are all going around behaving very differently towards each other and keep noticing the negative changes in each other and believing that you know why each other is behaving in this way. I had a new manager attempt to play this card with me from the day I walked in the door. They basically told me everything negative they could about everyone including their own Manager and even Managers who had left and ones I would never meet. I was basically told to not trust a single person who I worked with. "Welcome aboard, but do not worry I will be here to support, help, guide and protect you from all these evil Narcissists that surround you", but you know you can trust me, look how honest I am" Is what they may have well said.

Semper Letteris Mandate: This is the one rule that you only ever need to keep in mind when working alongside or for a Narcissistic Manager. Semper Letteris mandate, it is Latin for "Always get it in writing". If someone at work offers you anything, tells you or promises you anything, always get it in writing. Emails are your best line of defence with the Narcissistic manager and always will be. Otherwise, it is just words, hot air and you can prove nothing without solid evidence, ever. You have to be prepared to record everything that is important within a meeting and make sure that you cover yourself by not reacting to the things that you have been told unless there is solid "reality" evidence to support this. Always keep a diary of events, in which you record times, date and things said. Keeping a work diary is essential if you fear that you are being abused at work by a Narcissistic manager or colleague. A work diary can be a really helpful reference for later on, as a key tool for becoming aware of a Narcissist is distorting your reality. If you have something that you can refer back to, it will not only support your claim but will also reassure you that you are not losing your mind, when someone attempts to gaslight you. The number of people who I have advised to keep a diary after visiting me were amazed by how many times their Narcissistic manager disputed those things they had recorded. But what was worse, was their manager had then attempted to distort their reality to such a degree that they then disputed the things they had recorded. Some Narcissistic managers then accused those people who called out their poor behaviour of being emotionally unwell. If you start to keep a work diary and this is the case, then beware as you may have a Narcissistic manager on your hands. Always, always get it in writing.

The Narcissist Date: It is a real shame that dating in modern day society is littered with those with Narcissistic intent, if you are single and dating, you really need to be aware of the covert Narcissist and I will tell you why. The Narcissist loves and I do mean loves dating as it is fertile ground for them. Why is this you may think? Well, look at this from the Narcissists point of view. What if there was a place where a Narcissist could go to find people who were lonely, may be vulnerable, where you already knew what they wanted in advance (company, romance, love, a relationship). A place where you could chat anonymously and people would send you pictures of themselves, tell you all about their lives and what their hopes and dreams were and all you had to do was listen and say the right things to get what you wanted from them!!! Now if I said a place like this existed, how many Narcissists would literally queue up to go there. Well, these places do exist and they are called, "dating sites". Now do not get me wrong there are some genuinely really decent people on dating sites who want to find a partner for all the right reasons. But there are also a number of people on these sites who are predatory and just waiting for you to sign up. I could write a whole book on the perils and pitfalls of internet dating, but what we want to focus on here are Narcissists who we, unfortunately, end up dating. So how do you keep yourself safe while dating and looking out for Narcissists? Well, the first thing you need to aware of when dating is to keep yourself grounded and remind yourself that just because someone has paid interest to you, either online or in person that you still need to keep your feet on the ground. Romance, attraction and falling in love all ignite highly emotional states and if you are rushing ahead in your thoughts that this person is "The One" or "The only one like them, or "The only person for me", or any variation of this, then you are becoming over emotionally attached to them too quickly. This is your first step to spotting a Narcissist, as it keeps you grounded and not in a too highly emotionally charged state, which makes you vulnerable.

The next stage is to look out for the push-pull strategy, where they pay you loads of attention and then completely disappear, forcing you to chase them and then when you do, showing you once again with affection and then disappearing. We used to call this blowing hot and cold. You need to be aware of this tactic, as it keeps you circulating in high and low emotional states, this is where they want you to be, either chasing them or missing them. If these are the states your new date is putting you in, be aware and then start grounding yourself again. I know it can be tough, as every ping on your phone can signify a message from that new person and you feel the emotions rise. This is normal and it should feel that way, but at the same time as you are enjoying it, be aware that your decisions will be made on those emotions.

Be aware of the love bombers. This is very seductive and I was once love bombed by an online date for 48 hours, who after this period for no reason, disappeared and could never be contacted again. When you are love bombed, someone will attempt to build up that strong emotional romantic connection with you in such a short stage of time, hearts, flowers, chocolates, over-stated and emotional texts, calls and emails. They may turn up on dates, dressed to kill and say and do all of the right things, unfortunately, due to their inability to have or hold a normal relationship they will not be able to keep this up and when they have pressed every emotional button they can with you, they will then......vanish. This will leave you feeling totally high and dry and if you are not careful, their departure can leave you in such an emotionally dip that you almost feel as though you are hitting a stage of depression. Now while this may seem similar to the push and pull tactic, it is different as once they have gone, they are gone. It can last for a week or a month even and in this time, just be aware of what you are committing to. It is very hard to resist the advances of someone who seems just perfect and is able to keep delivering, but you have to keep your feet on the ground and realise that this is not reality. For the Narcissist, this is a strategy that they will employ to bring down your barriers straight away, they are killing you with kindness and when they have taken what they want from you, they will go and quickly move onto the next. When my experience of a love bomber came, they were close to confessing their undying love and affection for me by the second date, whilst still talking to other people on dating sites at the same time.

Complex Background and red flags: A friend once told me how they invited a date over to their house and they sat on their sofa and talked about how they suffered at the hands of their former partner. They then told my friend of further stories of a poor abusive relationship, after abusive relationship. My friend explained how they talked for over one hour nonstop, not pausing for breath or letting them interject for 1 hour. You try talking for one hour nonstop, it is not easy. After this, my friend noticed for the rest of the evening their date paid little or no interest in his life or even asked them anything about it. When he did speak they listened and then went straight back to talking about themselves. Anytime my friend interjected with a comment they just related everything back to themselves and their poor background. I asked my friend what they were thinking and they confessed that they just wanted to get them out of their house and send them on their way with my business card. This person was totally self-absorbed and could not be moved off this subject. Now they had the good sense to realise this and did not see them again as they did not feel that they were in the right place for a relationship. There are those who have gone through many painful experiences and are not yet fully recovered or healed from them, for many people it's not their fault, but they do need to take responsibility for their own recovery and rescue. Always be mindful of those who talk of complex and painful pasts, especially those who talk about years of constant abuse and do not appear to have let go of the pain and healed. It can often, but not always be the case that those with Narcissistic intent may well have been a victim of an abusive relationship themselves, or at least tell you they have. When I was talking to my friend, they explained the thing that really worried them about this person they dated was that they had a fascination for Narcissists, books, websites forums etc and said that these days they acted like a Narcissist towards their Narcissistic ex-partners. Never ignore a red flag, no matter how a person presents or messages you, this book will by now have given you a good grounding in what to look out for, but the important message here is to never ignore it, just for the sake of having a date or being in a relationship.

The Narcissist Friend: As I said earlier that word relationship can cover a multitude of sins. Well, the word friend can also get in there and do a lot of damage, especially when used by those who wish to manipulate you. I once knew someone who when I was young befriended people very, very quickly and before long was in every area of their lives. Initially, they were always there, supportive, helpful funny, life and soul of the party. They were practically like family and treated "themselves" as if they were, even turning up at meal times and referring to other family members as if they were family "Hi Mum, hello Nan". Is this person already starting to sound familiar to you by any chance? Look around are they sat on your sofa right now, helping themselves to your food out of the fridge, offering to house sit, helping with your wedding plans, no sorry taking over your wedding plans. In fact, doing anything they can to be useful to your world and life. It is very seductive when they turn up, they are godsends and you feel so lucky to have this bright, funny helpful upbeat person around. They will solve all problems, cure all ills and ask nothing in return, except to be part of your world. Then you one day when you are out together doing something together, they will lower their voice and say "I need to talk to you about something". You will listen intently and then they will say something like this "Have you ever noticed how whenever I am around, your friend (Insert your best friends name here) never talks to me, I don't think they like me". You might reassure them and they will then follow up with "It is probably after I overheard what they were saying last week and now they are worried that I am going to tell you". Boom, there you go they have reeled you in and hooked you, your new best buddy who does everything for you has just made the first crack in your friendship between you and whoever has spotted and suspicious of their real intentions. This is something that you need to be aware of with your new over enthusiastic and ever helpful pal. Someone in your group will spot the Narcissist for who they are and the game is on. This is the biggest red flag within any new "friendship" when someone sets out to destabilise all of your current and supportive relationships. It is the classic political and military strategy of cutting you off from others and for a Narcissist it serves a double meaning as it cuts you off from the reality of sensible and reasonable voices. Just think about how effective this is, first they get in, prove their worth, go beyond to help, form family bonds, use first and family name bias and then de-structure from within in. This tactic will not only be effective when used by the Narcissist new friend it will also be used by the Narcissistic over friendly manager and Narcissistic partner. It is so powerful when used by a friend as they can gift wrap it all in the world "Friend"

The Narcissist Family member:

So what do you do if you wake up and realise that you have a card-carrying Narcissist within your own family? Now I am not talking about your partner as we have covered that relationship in depth. I am talking about a brother or sister, uncle, aunt or even one of your parents. It happens and it is one of those things which we do not always wish to consider and that is Narcissists live within peoples families. We might think it unthinkable, but there are those who score high on the Narcissistic and high functioning scale, who are also parents, brothers, sisters or cousins to us. So what do you do if you are in a family relationship with someone who has Narcissistic tendencies? For a start, this is really difficult as you will have to acknowledge, that this is who they are and always have been and more importantly always will be. It is never comfortable to admit that this person who has been in your life is a Narcissist, but it will help to explain their behaviour and it will start to help you with how you feel about their behaviour towards you. You may have to seriously consider your approach to your relationship with them as in the past they may well have been the cause of some poor internal feeling for you due to their behaviour. Now I am not saying do not see the person again and actually, this is a major concern when you have a Narcissist within your household, as they may be unavoidable and not seeing them may not be an option. If this is the case then you need to manage and negotiate your time around them very carefully and start to think through your communication and what you decide to reveal to them. It is hard, really hard if you have anyone within your family, whom you think that you cannot trust. You have to remember that Narcissism crosses all boundaries and divides and once again it is being realistic about what you are ever going to be able to achieve within a relationship with them. Many people have asked me if they should confront family members and attempt to get them help. This is a really contentious point, as how do you approach a long term family member, who may be high functioning in many areas of their life and tell them that you have decided that they should change their ways? I have deliberately stayed away from the subject of supporting and helping Narcissists to see the error of their ways, as it is not the basis of the book. I have in all of my years of experience never encountered an EX Narcissist who has cleaned up their act because their brothers or daughter told them to. I have never had a Narcissist come to me for therapy and the only time I ever suggested to someone with high Narcissistic tendencies that attending therapy would be a good idea, they totally dismissed it out of hand. You see the problem is for a Narcissist to attend any kind of therapy is that they would have to acknowledge they were less than perfect. It would also mean that their behaviour would be highlighted and maybe suggested that it needs to be changed as it is wrong. As I said earlier if they have a perfect strategy for getting what they want, then why would they change it, ever? There are many things in life which can be altered, improved upon and developed. There are also some things in life that at best can just be managed effectively. An acute Narcissistic personality is one of those things that if you encounter, you can at best manage the situation and person by reading and studying the chapters of this book. With a Narcissist, you are talking about a person's conscious choice process here, not a random unconscious act or someone acting out of illness. I have not sugar coated Narcissism from my opening words and that is for a good reason, those with Narcissistic intent will harm others to achieve their goals. At best you can manage your communication, relationship and own feelings around them and if you are in an unavoidable relationship with a Narcissist you need to get good at the skills I mention and quickly. Always remember if you do not have plans for yourself then they will have plans for you. Sometimes there are no easy answers and heartbreaking as it is, we have to consider our own emotional health and survival even within a close family relationship

The Covert Narcissist. Like many subjects around Narcissism, the subject of covert Narcissists has been covered in depth. Covert Narcissists are amongst the most damaging of all, they can hide in plain sight, totally undetected for years and pass themselves off as the most genuine, decent and benevolent people you have ever met. They can ply their Narcissistic tradecraft as liberally as they wish, destroying lives and people in the process while they obtain whatever they like from those around them and seldom ever get caught. But why is this? The covert Narcissist hardly ever lets the mask slip; they never bare their teeth and can exude a total wide-eyed innocence to anyone who falls foul of their cruel manipulations. They are the hardest to spot and you will find many who have positioned themselves within a community who both love and adore them and would think it unthinkable that this person is capable of such acts of atrocity. The covert Narcissist does not just rely on the blind-eyed gullibility of others, they actually encourage it by spouting virtuous comments and performing perceived acts of kindness. "Aren't they kind" you will hear others say, "They do so much for the community" and those who speak out against them or attempt to reveal their true form will find themselves shot down by their numerous followers. They are masters of their manipulative art and you should never be taken in by them. These are the people who will always keep their own counsel and never truly really let anyone in and even if you think they have let you in, it will be to fool and beguile you. No one is all good and everyone has a slight shadow side, always be aware of those who bestow constant good virtues and never ever wish to show a less than pleasant side to their demeanour. You can often spot covert Narcissists, as like Narcissists they like to take centre stage, but will do it under the guise of being virtuous. They will often use the cause that they are seen to be promoting to further their own personal goals, as it is so much easier to control and manipulate others into doing their bidding if they feel that it is for the greater good. How difficult is it for someone to say no to someone who is asking for help for a "good cause". Always be aware of those people who do need to put themselves permanently in the spotlight of these good causes, there are many great people doing good work, who do not promote their own actions.

One of the most heartbreaking cases I can ever recall was someone who had come to see me in a very poor emotional state after their life had been almost totally destroyed by a most vicious Narcissist. The person whom they were close to had viscously destroyed their self-esteem, their levels of confidence and had done it over the course of a number of years, slowly but surely manoeuvring everyone against this person. But to the outside world the person who had destroyed them presented as kind, happy, caring, hardworking and benevolent. They were a true covert Narcissist in every sense of the word and were able to reframe a totally innocent person to everyone else, as someone they were not. In therapy, the person admitted to me that they were close to suicide due to the actions of this cruel and manipulative Narcissist and had felt that their only option was to just move away from their own town and start again. Meanwhile, the covert Narcissist was still loved and applauded by all for their generous nature and friendly attitude. But the worst part was that they felt they were the only person in the world who could see them for what they were. They described how this person had constantly browbeaten them, chipped away at them and finally publically humiliated them time after time. I remember them saying "They just seem to get away with it and everyone treats them like they are a rock star". This for many victims of a covert Narcissist is the worse part, it is hard enough for us to wake up to realising that a person is abusive and then stop making excuses for them. It is then made much worse by others not believing us and why when you think about it, why would people believe you, when the person you are attempting to expose exudes nothing but warmth and charm to the outside world? After several sessions, the person in question healed and regained their confidence back and started to see themselves as a strong and capable person again. They also let go of their past and the need to expose this person for who they truly are. This as I have said before this is often as good as it gets, If you spot a covert Narcissist, then your worst mistake will always be to attempt to unmask them. You will waste endless hours of your precious life and energy wanting everyone to know how badly they treated you, it is never worth it. Move away from them and regain yourself. When dealing with a covert Narcissist it is never a zero-sum game of winning or losing, they will think it is and that is why they will always be locked away within their own mindset. Let others discover who they really are for themselves as it is not your job to expose them. For living well to your highest goals and values should always be your pathway.

7. TOTAL FREEDOM FROM ABUSE

They are gone I thought, finally out of my life. I sat down and relaxed into my sofa and breathed a huge sigh of total relief. All was silent and it felt lovely, I was alone, totally alone and by god I was happy with it. I asked a question that I had asked of myself several weeks ago "How did this happen?" only this time I felt really good, I smiled to myself and realised that "I had my life back". But that question came back to me "How did this happen". I was asking myself how had I gone through that really painful period, that fear and anxiety of being out of my relationship and it was ok, it was better than ok it was great.

I was happy, happy to be single. But I could not work it out, what had changed and where had all the fear gone? Like anything else in life that we fear, I had suddenly realised that fear of something is 100 times worse than living it. I had allowed myself to be abused, financially and emotionally, as I was fearful of the consequences of losing a relationship, but here it was gone and I was in the middle of it and it was OK, Ha, it was ok to be on my own. Suddenly a huge surge of power and enthusiasm took over as I realised the power of no longer being emotionally dependent on a relationship. It was as if I had discovered how to turn base metals into gold, I examined any and every area of my life. If I was happy and content to just be and I could remember this, then it would be impossible for me to ever be abused again within a relationship. I was good as I am, I was enough and I was a whole and complete person. I was ready, but what was I ready for? Another relationship, no that is the big mistake we make, we always look to obtain that relationship status again. When you are single, everyone seems to think that you are just going through this waiting and healing period until you find someone again. When you have been a victim of abuse that is the biggest mistake you make ever. You have got your power and control back, but still look to get straight back with someone again, as society, your family friends and social media status says you should. But still, this question was burning in the back of my mind, "what happened and how did I get to this point" How did I get to this magical state of happiness and being "alone"?

Building and Crossing the bridge
Then the answer came to me, or rather the answers came to me. I got to this point, not just by doing one thing as there was not just one answer that made me feel my sense of self-worth again. It was many things that I did and they all counted. All of the small daily rituals and exercises that I have written about in this book and given to you were like bricks, solid bricks. But unlike many people I had not used these bricks to build a wall (building walls gets us nowhere) I had used my bricks to build a bridge and the bridge that I had built allowed me to cross over to a whole new state of being. I built my bridge pretty much by myself and then crossed it. Yes, there were others who were there along the way who kept me company and gave me so much support and I will always remember and value them, but I built this myself. It was my bridge and I had taken ownership of building it. I guess I had taken ownership of my own pain and suffering and decided that I needed to do something new.

I had found a place where I was untouchable, not inaccessible or cold and unemotional, but a place where I had come to know myself and what I wanted. So how do you do this, how do you get to this state where for you abuse is a thing of the past?

Practise and rehearsal: Every day, I used those positive techniques that would help my self-esteem and self-belief. I gave myself lots of positive self-talk and believed it. I lived life to my values and no one else's. This gave me back my important sense of self. This was to be my single status sense of self, where I acknowledged that no relationship was better than an abusive one.

I lived: Gym, movies, books, studying, friends, cooking, walking, cycling, writing, my career and family. I put my focus back into these important areas explored new thoughts about what I could do. I moved house, I stayed in London and studied. I met new people and took on new work roles. None of which relied upon me being in a relationship.

I changed my mind: Maybe singularly the most important thing that I did was to change my mind. I changed the way in which I thought. I was no longer an emotional reactionary person. I learnt how to just be, through calmness and meditation and this just gave me a great insight into other people. As they made more noise, I made less and listened like never before. As I became more aware of others, it became easier to spot Narcissistic people and their attempts at coercion and manipulation.

Finally back to the start
Then I had one final thought, it was my fault! It was all totally my own fault!! I had to admit it to myself, it really was my own entire fault that I had suffered at the hands of Narcissists, I just did not know it at the time and neither did you. I opened this book by telling you there are two reasons why you have ever been abused by a Narcissist and one of them is because you allowed it to happen. I allowed it to happen to me, I really did. I was a smart guy who knew stuff about the world and how people work, but I allowed Narcissistic people to manipulate me as I wanted to believe their lies and promises. They really are the Narc Side, they offer you quicker and more seductive options and routes for your happiness either in life, work career or relationships and I accepted their invitations and invited them freely into my world. Come on in let me tell you all my hopes,

dreams fears and phobias, so you can come and use them to abuse me. I wanted something, I wanted many things and they drew me pictures and told me stories of how they would get them for me and I believed them.

There are no short cuts in life and those who offer a quick route to happiness use this as nothing more than a tool to exploit you. You need to work hard, you need to make a strong effort at making sure you are safe and secure in your world against those who wish to exploit you. You need to prepare for war and it is a war and never ever trust anyone who tells you that it is not a war, it is. We are not programmed for war, so it is worth repeating that you need to be. You and your world are the casualties of this war, but only if you allow it to happen.

Now go back to the start of this book and do something really different. Read it again, read it two or three times to really learn all of those daily techniques that you need to master. Work through the things within the book, when you do, you will really be surprised with the answers and results and then in a few weeks work through them again and see where you are now.

But just for the moment, just for a while stop now and rest and take a moment. Breath in and out, it always starts with breathing (I know this, as I saw it in The Karate Kid). You have work to do, you may be about to go to war, or build a bridge to a new life where you are in control. Look for good people, they are out there and aim for those relationships that meet everyone's needs. But first, you need to be in that great relationship with, yourself. A relationship so good, that no matter what happens, you know you will always have it and it will always be there for you.

So, for now, I will end with these words.

Keep in touch with reality.
Never be taken in by words, only deeds and actions.
Stay emotionally centred and in control at all times
Question everything and everyone.
Always remember the wisest words of all,
You know nothing, about anyone or anything

Jason Edwards

Made in the USA
Middletown, DE
02 November 2023

41787672R00104